peter howard

SELECTIONS FROM A SERIES OF ADDRESSES BY
THE AUTHOR OF THE FOLLOWING:

BOOKS

INNOCENT MEN
FIGHTERS EVER
IDEAS HAVE LEGS
THAT MAN FRANK BUCHMAN
MEN ON TRIAL
THE WORLD REBUILT
REMAKING MEN
AN IDEA TO WIN THE WORLD
EFFECTIVE STATESMANSHIP
AMERICA NEEDS AN IDEOLOGY
FRANK BUCHMAN'S SECRET
BRITAIN AND THE BEAST
BEAVERBROOK

PLAYS

THE REAL NEWS
THE DICTATOR'S SLIPPERS
THE BOSS
WE ARE TOMORROW
THE VANISHING ISLAND
RUMPELSNITS
THE MAN WHO WOULD NOT DIE
MIRACLE IN THE SUN
PICKLE HILL
THE HURRICANE
THE LADDER
MUSIC AT MIDNIGHT
SPACE IS SO STARTLING
THROUGH THE GARDEN WALL
THE DIPLOMATS
MR. BROWN COMES DOWN THE HILL

FOREWORD BY HIS EMINENCE
RICHARD CARDINAL CUSHING
ARCHBISHOP OF BOSTON

 HENRY REGNERY COMPANY

D

design

for

dedication

* * *

HICAGO

Contents

ᴆᴅ

FOREWORD vii

INTRODUCTION ix

1 A FRESH LOOK AT FREEDOM 1

2 DEAD KNIGHT IN ARMOR? 17

3 THE NEW TYPE OF MAN 27

4 REVOLUTION OF CHARACTER 41

5 THREE PRONGS, OR FOUR 55

6 HEART POWER AND HATE POWER 63

7 TOMORROW'S AMERICAN 73

8 WHAT COLOR IS GOD'S SKIN? 95

9 LABOR CAN SHIFT THE NATION 107

10 CUBA COULD BE FREE 121

11 NOT BY WHEAT ALONE 131

12 DESIGN FOR DEDICATION 143

ASKED—AND ANSWERED 157

11516

Foreword

PETER HOWARD is a friend of mine. He is in charge of the program of Moral Re-Armament and well known throughout the world for his great and scholarly efforts in behalf of that noble cause. To his talent and training as a newspaperman he has added the moral insight drawn from experience with men in many lands.

He has made some of the finest addresses I have read in modern times. In these, reprinted in this present volume, he has stated old truths magnificently in their fresh relationship to the realities of today. To Americans, carrying a larger load of world responsibility than ever before in history, they point a leadership that could preserve faith and freedom for millions.

We can never influence the Communist world merely by showing how our democracy functions and how well off we are. Every Christian prays: "Thy will be done, on earth as it is in Heaven." It is nonsense to pray like that without seriously desiring what we are praying for.

If I really want it, then I must stand up for it, in my own life and in the life of others, in the life of the nation and in the life of the whole world, with all that I am and have, led by God, in community with others who feel the same obligation.

Then indeed the miracle will be achieved and other nations and peoples will be impressed. They will follow genuine moral leadership, not material progress.

That is ideology. That is Christianity. That is moral strength.

Speaking on March 4 of this year before the Massachusetts State Senate in an address which has given the title *Design for Dedication* to this book, Peter Howard said:

"We live in an age for heroes. No time has ever offered man such perils or such prizes. Man can either provide a full life for humanity, or destroy himself with the problems he has created. The test of this century will prove to be whether man matches the growth of wealth and power with the growth of spirit and character—or whether, like an infant heedlessly playing with terrible toys, he destroys the house he would have inherited.

"If America succeeds in creating the new type of man and the new type of society that the pace and pressure of the hour demands, she will lead humanity onward in the next stage of human evolution."

His words are a challenge for all. They bring an extraordinary clarity about America and the world that is most welcome.

Richard Cardinal Cushing

Archbishop of Boston

May 31, 1964

Introduction

THE SPEECHES of Peter Howard collected in these pages were delivered during a ten-week visit to the United States and Canada, between late December 1963 and early March 1964.

Mr. Howard made 46 speeches in 25 cities and 14 states. He traveled to the far corners of the country—the Pacific Northwest, Southern Arizona, Florida and New England. He spoke in the South and in the Midwest, as well as in Canada. He crossed the continent five times. In addition to the occasions referred to in these pages, he held press conferences, spoke on radio and television, conferred with State Governors, Canadian Cabinet Ministers, church leaders, and captains of finance, industry and labor. His words were carried by television from coast to coast in Canada and by radio to Cuba.

Peter Howard is an Englishman with an international reputation as a playwright, political columnist, author, sportsman, lecturer and farmer. Most men would be well content with the measure of success which he has achieved in any one of these varied endeavors.

Senate President John E. Powers, introducing Mr. Howard to the Massachusetts legislators before the address which concludes this volume, called him "one of the most remarkable men of this or any other era." He was described by the

Portland *Oregon Journal* as "a man who evidently knows the world situation better than we know the suburbs."

Mr. Howard's books have sold over four million copies. His plays have proved box-office attractions, and are currently being performed on five continents.

In the '30's Lord Beaverbrook made him his top political columnist. As co-author of the widely read book, *Guilty Men,* he is considered by many to have played a significant part in arousing British opinion against appeasement and preparing for the advent of Winston Churchill as war-time Prime Minister.

He played rugby football for England nine times in international matches and was a member of the British bobsled foursome which broke three world records at the Cortina International Championships in 1939. His wife is Doris Metaxa, Wimbledon tennis doubles champion in 1933-34. When he bought his East Anglian farm it was rated in the least productive category. Now it not only runs at a profit, but is visited by farmers from around the world who are interested in his methods.

It is fair to say that these achievements are of small significance to Peter Howard compared to the primary commitment of his life. He is first and foremost a revolutionary, wholly dedicated to the remaking of the world. His friendship for twenty years with Frank Buchman, Pennsylvania-born pioneer of Moral Re-Armament, led him to undertake a wide-ranging initiative in MRA's post-war world program. Since Dr. Buchman's death in 1961, there has been a vast acceleration in Moral Re-Armament's global advance, in which Peter Howard has carried a prime responsibility.

The onrush of national and world events which form the

background of his speeches has also had a sensational quality. Mr. Howard arrived in North America less than a month after the assassination of President Kennedy. He came from Asia, which had been deeply shaken by the death of President Diem. As the New Year unfolded, President Johnson had scarcely finished voicing optimistic words in his State of the Union message when American prestige suffered one hammer blow after another.

First came the ignominious deadlock with Panama; then the violent removal of United States officials from Zanzibar. Then, as Zanzibar was swiftly revealed to be an ideological Cuba for Africa, the new nations of Tanganyika, Uganda and Kenya were imperiled by the mutiny of their armies. Chou En-lai, on hand in Africa to seal the fate of these countries, was only frustrated at the last moment by Prime Minister Kenyatta's bold action in summoning British troops. The uneasy ties between America and the new African nations were also revealed in Ghana, where the Stars and Stripes was torn from the Embassy mast.

On top of this turbulence came the even greater crisis of Cyprus. And President de Gaulle chose this moment to dramatize these divisions still further by his recognition of Red China.

Meanwhile, across the globe in Asia the removal of Diem, which our press had implied would be a signal for brighter days in Vietnam, was in fact followed by worse military setbacks in the war with the Viet Cong and greater confusion in the country.

To the south, President Sukarno threatened violence against Malaysia so blatantly that Robert Kennedy was dispatched to smooth the dispute. His efforts were soon proved abortive as Indonesia moved steadily, with support from the

Communist powers, toward the take-over of Singapore and the wealthy resources of Malaysia.

As if this were not enough, the shaky neutralist game being played in Laos and Cambodia turned yet further against us; the illness of Nehru raised grave speculation as to the future stability of India; and Chou En-lai accomplished his diplomatic coup in the rapprochement of Pakistan and China.

In Latin America, Castro continued his program of infiltration and subversion; despite the ouster of Goulart, Brazil's future remained hazardous; national pressures in Argentina did not lessen following the seizure of American oil properties; only military control prevented anarchy in Paraguay and Ecuador as well as in Honduras and the Dominican Republic. Leftist terrorism continued in Venezuela and labor unrest in Bolivia.

The uncomfortable realities of the state of the world were somewhat blunted at home by predictions of a continued economic boom, and the tax cut added to the prospect of affluence. An election year, like Christmas, started earlier than ever, with endless discussions of political personalities and prospects.

Perhaps it was these superficial preoccupations which served to dull reactions to other urgent signs of the times— the Bobby Baker revelations of widespread corruption in high places, the recurrence of race violence, the swiftly mounting statistics of crime and immorality—all symptoms of a grave disorder in the character and society of the nation.

The words of Peter Howard cut across both the complacency and the defeatism of the American public. They are ablaze with the urgency of the age. They spell a revolt against the evils of our time and a challenge to turn the tide of history.

His audiences responded with standing ovations, question periods which would not end, and people who thronged around him long after the speaking was done.

These audiences, while unanimous in their response, were remarkable for their variety. They ranged from university professors to high school students, union officials to Wall Street bankers, liberal intellectuals to the conservatives of Palm Springs and Westchester. He spoke at a famous Catholic women's college in the East and before the student bodies of Lutheran and Presbyterian colleges in the West. He addressed on successive days social leaders of the white community of Atlanta and students of the Negro colleges of Morris-Brown, Morehouse, and Spelman in the same city. He was the guest of Governor Faubus of Arkansas and of Philander Smith College of Little Rock.

The speeches which follow contain illuminating and provocative facts and ideas. They diagnose the nature of the age in which we live and they expose the perils, the follies and evils we face. But pre-eminently they draw a "design for dedication" for every American who loves his country and longs to have a part in setting her on the high road of destiny for which God created her.

THE EDITORS

1

*"The multiplying strength,
wealth and power of the United
States is perhaps the greatest human
story of the ages. Certain it is
that the future of mankind depends
on where America is heading—
and if America knows where
she is heading."*

A Fresh Look at Freedom

Commonwealth Club,
San Francisco, California
February 28, 1964

IT IS NOT my purpose to try and coax America, from the platform of the Commonwealth Club, to rejoin the British Commonwealth of Nations. Such a plan would not succeed—and it would be disastrous for all of us if it did. The truth is that had your country and my own not enjoyed that family quarrel which led so many years ago to judicial separation, if not divorce, we in Europe would not be free today.

The multiplying strength, wealth and power of the United States of America after severance from Britain is perhaps the greatest human story of the ages. Certain it is that we owe our existing liberties to your blood, your valor and your gold. Certain, too, that the future history of mankind depends on where America now is heading—and *if* America knows where she is heading. Too often we have repaid your generosity with jealousy, your courage with criticism, your hand of friendship with an upturned and superior nose. For this I feel sorry.

Yet I happen to be a man proud of the British Commonwealth and of my country. At a time when patriotism seems out of fashion, I am a patriot. At a time when it is customary

1

to sneer at Imperialists whose boots went tramping so long over so large a section of this planet, I believe that in the light of history, the British people will be able to say that, despite failures of motive and frailties of selfishness, we did our best to elevate, educate, emancipate millions of our fellow men who otherwise might still be dwelling in huts and jungles, but who today stand in charge of mighty countries as free men.

I also believe that a growth in friendship and understanding between the English-speaking peoples is of importance if we are to secure peace and build a world that works. Now we British have an almost unconquerable longing to be loved. It is fair to say that we do not always achieve that aim. But, sadly, neither do Americans. President Johnson remarked the other day that America is a much-loved country in the modern world and that only belly-achers fail to appreciate her virtues. Alas! Belly-achers abound in Asia, through which I recently have made my tenth journey. Some of them also seem to have found their way to Washington, D.C. So what with the belly-achers and Bobby Bakers of life, President Johnson is afflicted with many needless burdens in the midst of his vast responsibilities.

There was a book called *The Ugly American.* I did not like the book. Much of it seemed to me unjust and untimely, but there was enough truth in it to make it damaging. I do not believe that the Lovely Englishman is the answer to the Ugly American. In fact, I do not think Englishmen are all that lovely—nor Americans all that ugly. But it is an outlook which some hold and which makes mischief.

Mr. Richard Crossman, a leading Socialist of Britain and likely to hold an important post in our Cabinet if a Labor Government comes to power, earlier this month told of a wartime episode from North Africa which is revealing. At that time Mr. Harold Macmillan, one day to be Prime Minister, was British political adviser to General Eisenhower. Mr. Crossman was a leading propagandist of the Allied war effort, and living in the Hotel St. George, Algiers. Mr. Crossman describes how Macmillan sent for him and said: "Remember when you go to the Hotel St. George, you will regularly enter a room and see an American colonel, his cigar in his mouth and his feet on the table. In front of him will be an empty in-tray and an empty out-tray. When your eyes get used to the darkness, you will see in a corner an English captain, his feet down, his shoulders hunched, writing like mad, with a full in-tray and a full out-tray, and no cigar.

"Mr. Crossman, you will never call attention to this discrepancy. When you install a similar arrangement in your own office, you will always permit your American colleague not only to have a superior rank to yourself and much higher pay, but also the feeling that he is running the show. This will enable you to run it yourself.

"We, my dear Crossman, are Greeks in this American empire. You will find the Americans much as the Greeks found the Romans—big, vulgar, bustling people, more vigorous than we are and also more idle, with more unspoiled virtues but also more corrupt. We must run A.F.H.Q. as the Greek slaves ran the operations of the Emperor Claudius."

They say on the continent of Europe that you can tell an Englishman anywhere—but you cannot tell him much. Mr. Macmillan, however, is a Scot. But the sort of attitude that the conversation recorded by Mr. Crossman, if accurate, represents has helped to create many modern difficulties.

In Algiers at about this time was an eminent French civil servant. When France fell, this man, under the Vichy regime, had with courage and skill helped to transfer French gold reserves out of German clutches into Allied hands in Africa. Mr. Morgenthau, as Secretary of the Treasury, came to North Africa. Mr. Robert Murphy was American Consul in Morocco. In his book, *Diplomat Among Warriors,* Murphy declares that Mr. Morgenthau intruded into foreign policy, not his domain, and adopted the same superior attitude towards that French civil servant as Crossman says he was advised by Macmillan to show towards Americans. Mr. Morgenthau successfully got the Frenchman fired from his job. Mr. Murphy, who tried with others to block this move, records: "It proved impossible to get this decision reversed in Washington, so we were compelled to inform French headquarters that the man who probably was their most effective civilian administrator in Algiers was unacceptable to the American government, and he was sidetracked." The name of that Frenchman is Maurice Couve de Murville. He is France's Foreign Secretary today. He is second in power only to President de Gaulle and exercises much influence upon him. He has not forgotten his treatment in North Africa.

It is impossible to comprehend the Asian scene without some comprehension of what makes De Gaulle tick. For one thing, many French people have never forgiven Britain for our refusal to surrender in 1940 when France fell. I was dining that fateful night in London with a well-known French diplomat. He buried his face in his hands and wept. He conceived it his duty to return to France and share the sufferings of his people under German occupation. He did so.

I said to him: "France will again be free. You can be certain that in one year, ten years, twenty years you will see your friends marching once more through liberated Paris. We will never surrender." My French friend even in that tragic hour was nettled by my confidence. He said: "You *must* surrender. You will have to do it now that France has fallen. You cannot continue." It tore his pride to think that the stupid Anglo-Saxons would fight on while the intelligent Latins faced the realities of life and death. If we had given in too, it would have been a salve to the conscience of the French.

I am no supporter of today's policies of President de Gaulle. He appears resolute to keep Britain out of the Common Market and to bring Red China into the United Nations. Many Englishmen would prefer him to switch these ploys.

But few attempt to understand the reason for his attitudes. I was listening a few days ago to an influential American discussing De Gaulle on a national radio program. I quote his words: "Now he (President de Gaulle) has the nerve to talk about Latin America. What is *he* doing in Latin America? He has no money to give there. He is just flexing his muscles and rocking the boat. Well, we have to deal with this man who thinks himself the big Charlie. It complicates matters." This sneering at De Gaulle, the effort to explain him as a vain man only eager to establish his own grandeur in Europe and the world, is condescending and cheap. Nor is it the truth. De Gaulle is a great patriot, a great European, a great lover of liberty and a great pragmatist. He remembers Yalta. There Roosevelt, Stalin and Churchill decided under pressure of war, without consulting the French, to hand over a hundred million Eastern Europeans to Communism. De Gaulle and the French had deep emotional ties with Eastern European countries like Poland and Czechoslovakia. They fear that under pressures of peace tomorrow, Britain and America may hand over two hundred million in Western Europe to Communism, as yesterday they handed over Eastern Europe.

De Gaulle does not trust my country, nor yours. He is unwilling to have an American or British finger alone holding the trigger of the bomb in Europe. He doubts whether any American President or British Prime Minister, suddenly faced with a Russian advance into Berlin or Western Germany, would be ready to hazard the instant desolation of San Francisco, Los Angeles, Detroit, Chicago, Washington, New York, London, Liverpool and Glasgow in order to stop them. De Gaulle wishes to have something in his own hand with which to defy and destroy any who threaten the broad plains and loved cities of his France from the East. He sees in Red China a rival to Russia in Eastern Europe. He is eager to take all pressures, except that of Russia, away from China. He wants to make friends with the Chinese so that they may feel free to remain glaring, yellow to red eyeball, at Russia. He may nourish hopes that one day the Red and Yellow giants may devour each other. How realistic his policy is I do not venture to suggest. How hopeful he can be of success in promoting disunity in the Communist world, from a free world divided in its own ranks, I do not venture to predict. But that these are the real motives of his present policy I have no shadow of doubt.

Today De Gaulle has his French fingers deep in the Asian pie. He advocates a policy of neutralization in Southeast Asia. Vietnam is at this time the hub of the wheel. When the test ban treaty was signed, Russia was one sponsor of the treaty. China opposed it. North Vietnam which, until that point, had with guile and smile managed to hold hands with Russia and China at the same time, was forced to a choice. North Vietnam decided not to endorse the atomic treaty.

Since then Moscow wanes, Peking waxes in the affairs of North Vietnam. And China has made the war in Vietnam central to her Asian strategy. She sees after Vietnam the deluge—Cambodia, Laos, Thailand, Indonesia, Malaysia, India. She sees herself the center of the earth, the traditional belief and training of old China, with her masses joined to the raw materials of Indonesia and perhaps the industrial might of Japan to form a Yellow Colossus of Communism.

Soon President Johnson may be forced to grave and agonizing decisions. De Gaulle believes that the war in South Vietnam cannot be won under existing conditions where the West plays to the rules of the 1954 Geneva Treaty which split Indo-China, while Ho Chi Minh from the north breaks all the rules. Ho is sending in arms and trained troops through the jungle trails of Cambodia, and by boat to the Viet-Cong controlled beaches of the ocean, while political and military control of the Viet-Cong is maintained by radio from Hanoi in North Vietnam.

If the present Saigon regime is threatened with disintegration, America will have to decide whether to withdraw, to fight an all-out war, or to institute reprisals against the North Vietnamese intervention. Such reprisals might involve the bombing of selected targets in North Vietnam. And if the Chinese intervene, which would mean the Yellow Communists were ready to risk war with the U.S.A., it would, in the words of one Washington policy-maker, offer "a heaven-sent opportunity to hit certain targets in China." These targets are, of course, the Chinese atomic plants.

For beneath the broil and bubble on the surface of world affairs, the deeper currents have turned against the risk of thermo-nuclear war. Unless lunacy leads towards unilateral disarmament or to a wanton spirit of preventive war, the risk of nuclear conflict is not likely to become imminent until China has its own nuclear weapons and delivery system. According to Washington, that day is far off. According to Japanese Intelligence, it could happen within two years.

In these circumstances, the death of Diem may have been a costly miscalculation. On my recent journey through Asia, in different countries, in different cities, and in different languages, people asked: "Do you believe violence is a legitimate means of obtaining political ends?" They meant: Could they use force to destroy capitalism—should they kill rich men? When I replied that this seemed to me a bad plan, with one accord these Asians asked: "What about Vietnam? America showed us there that she now is ready to encourage violence in order to achieve her political purposes in another country." I do not say this is just. I do not say it is true. I do say it is a view running like a prairie fire through millions of hearts in Asia, Africa, Latin America today.

I do not express views for or against Diem's policies in Vietnam. He had his follies and his weaknesses. He had his difficult relatives. Most of us do. I can say from knowledge of the man that the stories that he was some kind of a Fascist beast living in the midst of a corrupt regime, among people who hated him, are a lie. The story was told to the American people that there was a persecution of Buddhists. News that pagodas were being closed hit the headlines here on August 21, 1963. The fact is that out of 4,000 pagodas in the country, twelve were closed on that day. Buddhist priests, punjis, have informed the press since Diem fell that not one Buddhist was killed during the closing of the pagodas.

David Halberstam of *The New York Times,* a newsman whose pen played a powerful part in molding the attitude of America towards Diem, said after Diem fell: "The Buddhist campaign was always political. This was a political dispute under a religious banner." Diem believed, and this has been confirmed by Buddhist leaders since the coup, that there had been Communist infiltration in certain Buddhist circles inside Vietnam.

Since Diem fell, seven other Buddhists have tragically immolated themselves in and around Saigon. Nothing, or very little of this, has reached the Western press, though before Diem's fall the punjis who poured gasoline over themselves and burned themselves to death were heralded everywhere as a symbol of the rebellion of tortured people against a cruel oppressor. But as Roger Hilsman, until three days ago Assistant Secretary of State for Far Eastern Affairs, said: "After the closing of the pagodas on August 21, the facts became irrelevant." On August 24 the State Department, without the knowledge of Secretary McNamara or of C.I.A. Director John McCone, sent instructions to Ambassador Lodge to unleash the Vietnamese rebel generals and destroy the Diem Government.

Hilsman now says there will be no neutralization of Vietnam. McNamara says he will "take all necessary measures to prevent a Communist victory in Vietnam." It will be interesting to observe what measures are taken short of all-out war.

It is worth taking one glance at Trich Tri Quang, the Buddhist leader who was granted political asylum by the Americans, and who engineered the anti-Diem campaign. He saw all the pamphlets and leaflets distributed during those days of violence against Diem. His was the master-hand behind the curtains. Trich Tri Quang was twice arrested by the French, when they were in control of that part of the world, for dealing with the Communists. By his own admission he is a member of the Viet-Minh Communist Liberation Front. His brother is currently working with Ho Chi Minh in the Viet-Cong's Ministry of the Interior. Interviewed by Marguerite

Higgins (*America,* January 4, 1964) shortly before Diem's death, the Buddhist leader said: "The current disorders could lead to Communist gains." He said his preferred solution for Vietnam was neutralism, adding: "We cannot get an arrangement with the North until we get rid of Diem and Nhu."

At this moment, in paddy fields and swamps, jungle darkness, slime, stench and mud of fetid rivers, Americans, Vietnamese, villagers and soldiers are putting to the test with their blood and suffering whether freedom shall or shall not endure in Vietnam. Without expressing views about the policies or character of Diem or the Nhus, one thing is certain. The United States, for the first time in the history of the country, encouraged the overthrow in time of war of a duly elected government fighting loyally against the common Communist invader. The bill for that deed has yet to be presented. But it will have to be.

Meanwhile Chou En-lai is returned from his African visit. He has announced that the continent is ripe for revolution and that all must now unite against America, the great Imperialist enemy.

The truth is that Chou En-lai stubbed his toe in Africa. Chou tripped unexpectedly over the character of one man. His name is Jomo Kenyatta.

They say Chou En-lai planned to make a triumphal entry into the United Socialist Soviet states of East Africa. That plan failed, although there were mutinous incidents in Tanganyika, Uganda and Kenya following the Communist coup in Zanzibar. Zanzibar has become Chou En-lai's Cuba in Africa, just as Mr. Khrushchev has his Cuba for Latin America. And by the way, watch Cyprus and Ceylon in this developing island strategy of world Communism.

But Chou En-lai had to cut short his African honeymoon.

For Kenyatta of Kenya did what few men expected him to do. In spite of the past record of Mau-Mau, in spite of hard things that had been said and done on both sides, he pocketed his pride and without consulting his Cabinet asked the British to send troops to maintain the freedom of Kenya. He encouraged Mr. Nyerere of Tanganyika and Mr. Obote of Uganda to do the same. They had sense enough to accept his advice. We British sent troops to the danger areas, though it is not easy politically to play the part of policeman in nations that so/recently rejoiced so loudly at your departure.

We left Zanzibar under great pressure from the United Nations and the United States. I think it was sincere pressure, but who has got in there? I want to quote you what Sheikh Kassim Hanga, who is the Prime Minister of Zanzibar, said. He, by the way, went to Moscow, where he was given a degree in economics at Lumumba University. He had tried for some time to get a degree in economics in London. He did not get a degree in London. This is what he said to a friend of mine in Zanzibar a month ago: "The Russians look after people who visit them, whereas the West just let us fend for ourselves." That is an indictment of London, my home town.

Prime Minister Hanga has a Russian wife, a pupil of the professor who architects Soviet policy in Africa. His colleague is a man called Sheikh Mohammed. He is the Foreign Minister of Zanzibar. They call him "Babu." He has had money from China and from Russia. He said this to the same friend of mine about the same time: "In Russia I feel no dynamism. The revolution has lost its momentum. But in China it is on the move. Everyone is behind it."

Sir Roy Welensky, a man of the Right, says that Russia has fifty per cent won the ideological war in Africa. All the new nations are non-aligned. If there is a showdown between East and West, that means no manpower, no materials, no bases in Africa for the free world. Trade unions in the emergent countries are mostly affiliated with the Communist-controlled World Federation of Trade Unions in Prague. That gives the Soviets a chance to operate legitimately inside the emergent African countries. And, of course, thousands of young Africans are given free university training in Moscow and are now pouring back into Africa. All right, get rid of the old Imperialists. But are we handing Africans over to freedom?

There is another point to ponder. In the Middle East lies a state called Israel. It is surrounded by the Arabs. Supposing we get in Africa an Arab north hostile to Israel and a black mid-continent, because it is Communist, hostile to the United States. This is a serious challenge.

Beware, lest in our desire to curry favor with emergent people, we promote every revolutionary into a George Washington when he may prove to be another Castro or Chou En-lai. Castro could never have taken Cuba without the backing of free men. Chou En-lai and Mao Tse-tung could never have taken China without the backing of free men. Sukarno could never have taken Indonesia without the thrust of free men.

I want to say something about President Sukarno because I am asked a great deal about him. The United States was keen to get the Dutch out of Indonesia. Out they went. I have talked with New Guineans who have now gone back into what they regard as slavery. They hated the Dutch. But when I talked about America, they said: "Those people, without consulting us, handed us over to a tyranny that in our view made the Dutch seem like a kindergarten." That is New Guinea.

In the free world some take the view that Sukarno is the

best block against Communism in Asia. There is a plan called Maphilindo—that is, a union of Malaysia, the Philippines and Indonesia. Sukarno says he will not play ball with that concept so long as Malaysia is a "puppet of British colonialism." I do not speak here on behalf of Britain. We made mistakes in our colonial rule. But we did our best.

Are we sure of Sukarno? We British are urged to sever our allegiance to Malaysia if the Maphilindo concept is going through. Sukarno will be top dog. Then what about Singapore? It is worth considering.

The moral and spiritual attitudes, the character and conduct of the free world are directly related to our success or failure in the cold war. Strength and wealth, bombs and dollars are essential to the survival of liberty. I pray no nation in our time will equal or surpass this country in military or money power. But in the long run democracy is neither stronger nor weaker than those who speak and live in her name. It is the character of the free peoples of the world that will decide whether freedom captures Communism, or whether Communism captures and abolishes freedom.

Lenin was perfectly aware of this truth when he said: "Our morality is wholly subordinate to the interests of the class struggle." By this he meant that what suits the convenience of his crowd is right and what does not suit them is wrong. It was an abandonment of absolutism in morality. If we in the free world yield the absolutism of our pristine convictions, if we abandon the code of conduct that the men who built America accepted as right, then wittingly or unwittingly we play the game of Communism.

Mal Whitfield, the great Olympic Gold Medalist, a Negro, who worked for seven years with the State Department in

Africa and elsewhere, understood this fully when he said: "The sex-mad Americans are ruining us in Africa. The impurity in the Americans is in direct proportion to the United States policy not working in Africa today."

Unhappily, some members of the British Foreign Office and of the U.S. State Department fail to grasp this central reality of our times. Some of them even have the folly to attack and assault with secret smear men in the free world who try to cure the moral compromises that are freedom's greatest weakness. They have the effrontery to call it anti-American, or even Communist or Fascist, if you love your country and mine enough to refuse to tolerate the intolerable, and to dare to cure what can be cured.

Of course in some cases this smear, this modern witch-hunt, this Goebbels technique of character assassination, may be projection. You all know the story of the two old ladies and the bottle of champagne. They had never drunk champagne before. They bought a bottle. At the end of the second glass one turned to the other and said: "My dear, you must be drunk. You have two noses." Sometimes I recall this when I hear the cry of "Communism" or "Hitlerism" raised from Downing Street, London, or Washington, D.C., against those in our society who try to cure the causes of Hitlerism or Communism. For of course decadence, corruption, deviation, compromise, immorality all through history have been the grave of freedom and the launching pad of Stalins and Hitlers. In other cases, it may simply be the reaction of guilty men whose consciences are stung and who desire to debase free society until it becomes more comfortable for them to live in.

I have high hopes for the future. I believe that truth will prevail and that there is a decency and integrity in the heart of ordinary people everywhere which will refuse to see our world overcome by the destruction of dictatorship or the death of atomic blast.

My faith is that America, with the glory of her past and the generosity and vigor of her present, will in the coming years grow to a giantdom of the spirit which will secure the peace and build a new world for herself, for her allies and, in the long run, for the whole bewildered, agonized, long-suffering but fundamentally noble humanity.

2

*"It would be an irony indeed if,
at the very time a great crack
appeared in the steel fabric of the
Communist world, free men
destroyed themselves with the very
materialism they so hate and
fear in their enemies."*

Dead Knight in Armor?

Town Hall,
Los Angeles, California
February 4, 1964

ONE MAN stands at my side as I speak. He is my young and
only brother, John. He fought through the last war in Africa,
in frozen islands of the Arctic Seas, on blood-soaked moun-
tain slopes of Italy, amid the heat, flies and fury of North
Africa, finally dropping with the paratroops at Arnhem,
where death met him. Like millions of others he gave life so
that we could inherit freedom. This freedom, dearly bought,
is dear to me.

Elsewhere men no longer enjoy the right to speak as their
conscience tells them. They are gagged. If they say what they
like when they like, they risk the terrors of a secret police. So
let us cherish freedom of speech and use it to the full in lands
where it yet remains. I shall have more to say on this ere I
finish.

It is hard for a foreigner to speak to America. We owe our
liberty to your muscle, blood and treasure. We know, too,
we owe our future liberty to America. America is going to
lead the earth forward in the right direction, or we will be
forced far in the wrong direction by other powers.

America is a giant Father Christmas staggering through

Asia, Africa, Latin America with a pack of goods, handing out gifts to the children, behaving with a generosity never before shown in the history of man. The children grab the gifts, scream for more, pick the pocket of Santa Claus as he passes by, try to trip him up, knock him down, abuse him and destroy him. It is a puzzle and a paradox. In the short time at my disposal, I mean to tell you why it has come to pass.

America needs an aim for humanity. She needs an idea in her head and an answer in her heart, as well as a pack of gifts on her back, a roll of dollars in one hand and a holocaust of bombs in the other. I thank God on my knees each day for the strength of America. I pray no country ever in my time or the time of my children and their children equals that strength. But without a revolutionary plan in which all men can share, without a faith which all can understand and love, without a self-discipline to match that plan and faith, America may become a dead knight in armor.

Moscow and Peking are planning day after day for Mr. U.S.A. Mr. U.S.A., what is your plan for Peking and Moscow? Is this country planning intelligently to take over the Communist world, to enlist the whole earth in its next forward step where the contradictions of the century are resolved and the hates, fears and greeds that divide and bedevil us are answered?

A Russian diplomat, believed by the F.B.I. to be one of the most skilled Communizers in this country, said to me not long ago at an Embassy party: "We in the Soviets have this great advantage. We have a strong ideology out to change the shape of the world. You in the West have no ideology." Talk about free enterprise and our way of life does not create an ideology. Nor is capitalism the answer to Communism. Capitalism is a social and economic system, and in my view a good one. Communism is a bid backed by the muscle, mind and money of colossal states to capture the allegiance and change the nature of mankind. Communism is far more than forcefully making fat men thin, and thin men fat.

In a Soviet textbook on psycho-politics, introduced by a speech from Beria, formerly head of the Secret Police, the Communist creed about the nature of man is set forth in these words:

> "Man is an animal. He is an animal which has been given a civilized veneer. Man is a collective animal grouped together for his own protection before the threat of his environment. Those who so group and control him must then have in their possession specialized techniques to direct the vagaries and energies of the animal man towards greater efficiency in the accomplishment of the goals of the State."

In other words, the State can use slaughterhouse, torture chamber, lash and whip to control the zoo over which it presides.

I hate McCarthyism. I loathe the sly innuendo about Communism, the private sneer, the public assassination of the character of anybody who dares to stand for the rights of the poor, the underprivileged, those of different color, class and background, in your country and in mine.

I am utterly opposed to a spiritual Gestapo and witch hunters who poke and pry into the private life of the individual. But I am also bound to say that I think public men should live lives beyond suspicion. Nobody forces a man into public life, but if he chooses to serve the public, then his private life no longer remains entirely his own affair. Freedom is as strong as the men who speak in her name.

But I truly believe the late Senator McCarthy has proved himself the Reds' best friend. He is the strongest ally the Communists ever had in America. Memory of his methods, or a distortion of them, have been used to cow and silence any who dare to believe that Communist-inspired men and issues still threaten America.

Let me quote the words of Mr. Henry J. Taylor, former U.S. Ambassador to Switzerland, published on January 24, 1964. He is a man whose integrity, so far as I know, has been unchallenged by Democrat or Republican. He says:

"Starting with the Bay of Pigs, after new teams entered the innards of the State Department and C.I.A., the endless pattern of surprises and failures would be utterly impossible unless our government had been infiltrated at the policy level.

"The British, French, West German, Italian, Dutch and Swedish governments have experienced such Soviet infiltration.

"As our American Ambassador to Switzerland, I saw this happen even there. And we are seeing the success of deep-cover Sino-Soviet agents and fellow travelers planted here.

"But all legislation and other important duties fall to nothing compared with the heart-breaking, shifty, diabolical problem President Johnson confronts: The restoration of internal top-level security.

"Moreover, he knows the enemy's self-serving alibi of 'witch hunt' will automatically blare, as always and everywhere, the moment he moves.

"May all intelligent citizens and thoughtful newspapers across our country help give him the strength to reach each discoverable truth, place security above every other consideration and let the chips fall where they may. This nation is in absolute peril—within Washington."

What can America say to the world? The truth is that God gave Britons and Americans two ears and one mouth, presumably intending that we should listen twice as much as we talked. But we have used our mouths so ceaselessly to tell other nations what to do, where to go, and how to behave that we have almost stopped being willing to listen to our friends and to learn from the footsteps of history. It does not impress the modern world when we tell everybody else unendingly how to live and what to do, but ourselves continue to live as we please. What we are shouts louder than what we say.

Such materialism is the driving force of the philosophy of Karl Marx. It would be an irony indeed if, at a time when a great crack appeared in the steel fabric of the Communist world, free men destroyed themselves with the very materialism they so hate and fear in their enemies.

A Latin American Consul in this City of Los Angeles said the other day: "I love North America, but in Mexico City we call your embassy 'the fairy palace.' Moral compromise in your State Department is running Latin America into the arms of Red China." When a C.I.A. man was told of the scandals caused in New Delhi by some of the drunkenness and womanizing of American Air Force men there, he said with indignation: "Those boys are patriots. They are pulling the bacon out of the fire for the Indians. The least the Indian Government could do for them is to give them women and drink." It may be the least that the Indian Government could do for them, but it certainly is the last thing that the Indians expect from nations that they wish to admire and love.

To America I say this: Freedom is in danger. Defend it with all your might. Defend it with all the power in your hand, and all the wisdom in your head and heart.

I read in *The New York Times* of Thursday, January 23, that the Federal Communications Commission refused to censor radio programs which sponsored Communist causes, perversion and sexual deviation of all kinds. They felt it would interfere with liberty and be contrary to the First Amendment of the Constitution to place any check or halt on this kind of program being sent into the homes of you and your children. If men are free to broadcast this sort of stuff, we must remain free to talk of purity, honesty and moral responsibility. It is not for me to say to America what subjects can and cannot be discussed in public and in private. I only know this. If we try to curb God in our gatherings as we curb dogs on our streets, we are on the road to tyranny.

You print on your money the proud boast: "In God We Trust." Does this make the dollar a religious emblem? It means, I suppose, that you expect Americans young and old to trust more in God than in money, sex, personality or any other factor of life. I cannot tell if *Time* magazine's recent picture of the sex life of America is accurate. It was certainly stimulating. But I do know that a society which glorifies free love and homosexuality will not last long as the home of the free.

I read in *The New York Times* of December 31, 1963, that by 1966 half the population of this country will be under 25 years of age. Two days later in the *Los Angeles Times* I read that J. Edgar Hoover says the Communist Party of America is planning for American youth. Their leaders formed final plans in Chicago, according to Hoover, last

October. Already a strong swing Leftwards is noted in American youth and in society.

This does not mean that all American youth are going to join the Communist Party. It does mean that an intelligent attempt is being made so to saturate the rising generation with Communist-inspired issues that by the time they take their place as leaders of communities, their whole outlook will be slanted in a direction unfavorable to American democracy.

Between the years 1961 and 1962, $28,962,000,000 was spent on education in this country (this figure comes from the United States Office of Education in Washington). For every dollar spent on education in 1962, $1.11 was spent on crime. Venereal disease among adolescents rose 130% between the years 1956 and 1961. To take a few cities as examples: Between 1955 and 1959, venereal disease rose 318% in New Orleans, 591% in San Francisco, 378% in Houston, 291% in Los Angeles, 280% in Washington, D.C. The illegitimacy rate has tripled since 1953. By 1970, ten million Americans will have been born out of wedlock. Forty per cent of the unwed mothers are between the ages of 15 and 19. And illegitimacy among 15- to 19-year-olds has increased 108% since World War II.

America stands before the world for man's undeniable right to life, liberty and the pursuit of happiness. If we turn life into the *dolce vita,* liberty into license to create a sex-centered, money-minded, drink-sodden, man-worshiping community, the pursuit of happiness into the pursuit of self-ishness as normal, expedient, even virtuous, then we shall condemn future generations to the loss of that freedom you and I inherit.

I love freedom. And I love America as I love my own

country. I will lay down my life, I will spend such fortune as I have, I will sweat and strive and pray and work and struggle to secure the future of this country. For I know that if America fails, the world fails. But America will not fail. She dare not fail. I have enough faith in the common man in this country to remain convinced that he will rise to the challenge of our times.

3

"We face a Red Age of tyranny,
a Dead Age of destruction, or an
age of a new type of man as different
from the Stone Age man,
the Steel Age man, the Dollar-
and-Sex Age man, as a Spaceman
is different from a man with
a wheelbarrow."

The New Type of Man

The Rotary Club,
Chicago, Illinois
January 14, 1964

HOPE remains untaxable even in my country. So I declare to you today that I am full of hope.

I have faith that the common man will rise to the challenge of our times. I have faith that America will create the new type of man able to live sanely with the secrets of wealth and power that his brain has torn from the earth and atom. We face a Red Age of tyranny, a Dead Age of destruction, or an age of a new type of man as different from the Stone Age man, the Steel Age man, the Dollar-and-Sex Age man, as a Spaceman is different from a man with a wheelbarrow.

I thank God night and morning for the wealth and strength and the generous vision of America. There has been nothing like it in the whole long story of humanity. But I also know that unless America discovers and proclaims a larger revolutionary aim, the whole earth may be enslaved or destroyed. And the whole earth includes America.

Let me read you quotations from the speeches of two men. Here is the first quotation:

"I am not referring to the absolute, infinite concepts of universal peace and goodwill of which some fantasies

27

and fanatics dream. . . . Let us focus instead on a more practical, more attainable peace—based not on a sudden revolution in human nature, but on a gradual evolution in human institutions."

The second quotation is as follows:

"Human beings must not act like animals. Man's conscience is most important. And the need is for everyone to be sensibly aware of satisfying the spiritual and material demands of human beings."

The first quotation I gave you was made by the late President Kennedy, speaking on June 10, 1963. The second quotation which said that man's conscience was most important was in Mr. Khrushchev's remarks given on December 30, 1963.

It is a paradox of our times that the Communist world, which for years has pursued a godless, materialistic path, now finds itself confronted with the need for a type of man which changed environment alone has not created. At the same time, in our free countries traditional moralities are under assault. Nations which in the past based their nationhood on a trust in God, and even printed the token of such trust on their money, now tend to become cynical and to think that materialism and material environment alone will achieve the purposes of humanity.

The concept that only a change in environment will change the nature of man is nothing short of old-fashioned Marxism, which most people would agree is already outmoded.

I have just come from Asia. That continent is trembling on the brink of dictatorship and war. At the same time, there are signs of a change that could bring hope to democracy and freedom.

Last year in India, 63% of the income tax was unpaid. That is the statement of Krishnamachari, the Finance Minister. Last year over $6,000,000 of unpaid fares were discovered on the national railways. And probably a far larger sum, the loss from those who traveled without taking the trouble to pay, was never discovered. An Indian industrialist told me that it is impossible to do business in India today without corruption among Government and Civil Service. He said that if you were honest in business, you would go out of business. At the same time, the Indian House of the People had passed a law saying that any director of any corporation can be removed by Government decree without any reason given, and replaced by a Government nominee.

In this situation, Rajmohan Gandhi, grandson of Mahatma Gandhi, is calling for a moral revolution to answer the corruption and disintegration that threaten his land. He has met with an overwhelming response. Mr. Nehru told me in Delhi in November that Gandhi has achieved a contact with the youth of India which Indian leaders and Cabinet Ministers, for the last five years, have lost. Gandhi has asked for 10,000 young Indians to give their lives with him for the moral rearmament of the country. In the first four weeks of his appeal he received the names of over 4,000. City officials in Delhi have been paying back the money they received as bribes. University students have been going to the presidents and faculties describing how they have cheated in their examinations, and asking that for the sake of India, the colleges shall now be cleaned up.

President Prasad of India told me last time I saw him that

the work Gandhi was doing was in his view the most important event happening in India today.

American youth have also begun to rise to the challenge
of our times. I have just seen out on the West Coast a force
of young Americans, led by the son and daughter of the
Executive Director of the National Academy of Sciences in
Washington, who have enlisted students and others to give
the right moral and ideological leadership to the youth of
America. They have written a play called "Across the River"
which is being shown nightly in Los Angeles. Students from
the great colleges and the high schools come to see it. Many
of them are changing. They are becoming honest with their
families, and beginning to dedicate their lives to secure the
freedom that they have inherited and make it safe for their
own children when they have them. They plan to take this
play, if they can raise the money, to the different colleges
and states of America. They want to get it filmed. They aim
to raise 10,000 American youth to stand with them in this
supreme task. They aim to do for the United States what so
far the State Department has failed to do, namely, to enable
American youth to speak to Russian or Chinese youth in such
a way that they can be won to a greater concept and a
sounder, more revolutionary plan for the future of the world.

I want to quote you three great experts on democracy. The
first is Lenin. He was out to destroy democracy. He said:
"Our revolution can never succeed until the myth of God is
removed from the mind of man. Our morality is wholly subordinate to the interests of the class struggle." By this Lenin
simply meant that what suited the Communist cause was
right, and what did not suit it was wrong. And naturally if we
in free society adopt the same moral code as Lenin, and if we
live proclaiming a faith in God but do not make that faith so

real that it affects our home life, our industrial life, and our relationship with other nations, then whether we like it or not we shall be playing the Communist game.

The second expert on democracy I want to quote is Hitler. He also hated democracy. He was one of the most violent anti-Communists that ever lived, but only succeeded in spreading Communism halfway across the globe and killing himself in the process. In a set of directives from the Gestapo he instructed the Nazi military authorities to smash Moral Re-Armament wherever they found it, as a force which was restoring conscience to humanity. He accused MRA of "lending the Christian garment to world democratic aims." It was an interesting observation from that notorious oppressor of minorities and enemy of freedom.

The third expert on democracy was an American. His name was William Penn. He gave utterance to a truth which I believe is not religious, but everlasting political wisdom. He said: "Men must choose to be governed by God or they condemn themselves to be ruled by tyrants." By this he simply meant that the way men conduct themselves with each other decides whether they will remain free or whether the strong man will step into control. It is true in a home, or a nation. I know lots of homes in my country where everybody talks about tolerance, free enterprise, and democracy, but where there is a strong dictatorship either from mother or father, and a lot of Communist kids in revolt. I know of countries in Europe where there has been much talk of liberty but where the division, hatred, and selfishness have led to such disintegration that dictatorship has taken over.

Many people during my present visit to America have asked me about certain Supreme Court decisions. Of course, it is not my job to question the Supreme Court. I do thank

God for a country where justice still prevails and is known to prevail. But I would like to say to you today that no decision of any Supreme Court can keep you or me or our country from a belief in a Supreme Being. No legislation can rob me of my faith. No law can prevent me from obeying the dictates of my heart and conscience. The future of America depends, in my view, not on a decision of any Supreme Court, but on the decisions of millions of Americans.

I speak to you today in the heart of America. Chicago is indeed the heartbeat of the industry that is your nation's strength. May the hammer strokes of this mighty heart beat out a song that is heard around the waking world. May the industrial heart of the United States become the ideological heart of a united humanity. May this amazing land that has taught humanity in the past the secrets of liberty, the secrets of living with a comfort and a genius that men have never known before, now take up the task of teaching all men how to live.

God keep America strong and great so that humbly, hopefully, passionately she takes up the task of remaking the world and leads mankind once more into the path of sanity and lasting peace.

Banquet given by The Honorable Samuel W. Yorty
Mayor of Los Angeles
January 3, 1964

I HAD MEANT this evening to speak courteously, as far as an Englishman can be courteous, to thank you all for your bounteous hospitality—Americans are the most generous people in the world—to tell you what we owe to your country, and to sit down. But I am going to do something far more controversial and dangerous. I am going to tell you the truth, as if this might be the last time we met, and as if it were the last thing I would say.

I want you to put the clock of modern life forward twenty, thirty, fifty, a hundred years. In my lifetime, the clock of industry and technology has gone forward to an extent people do not comprehend at all. We read about space. We read about atomic destruction, which the Japanese have described but which apparently we know very little about. We read about guided missiles, electronics, and transplanting organs from one person to another, living or dead. We live amongst it and we don't regard it. It just passes us by like a cloud of feathers in a snowstorm. And we still maintain the old hates —color, race, class, management and labor—that inevitably must destroy the world unless we keep pace with the march of technology in industry.

Man has become a phenomenal industrial giant. It is possible now in the modern world to feed everybody. It is possible to give everybody a decent home to live in. It is possible for everyone everywhere to have a chance in life whatever their background and education. What stops it? The old-fashioned fear and hate and greed in the human heart. Unless America comprehends that, and with all its will and discipline says, "We will stride ahead and put the clock forward so the whole of humanity together can take the next step in human evolution," the world is going to destroy itself. As sure as I stand here we are going into a new dark age of slavery that will make Hitler look like Mickey Mouse—or we are going into atomic war.

I don't myself believe any nation has the strength or genius to accomplish this except America. I would like to think my country did. I think we have made certain contributions. I don't think our contributions are ended. But America happens to be the strongest country in the world. It happens to be the richest country in the world. And it happens to have still the spirit of adventure—not lively but still flickering—in the hearts of most of its people. That is our hope.

Mr. J. Edgar Hoover says that there is a strong swing to the left in American youth. He says it is a swing planned by the Communist Party. If Mr. Hoover's advice had been heeded, certain events would not have taken place in Dallas. Don't let us be too sure we know better when a man like Hoover comes forward with a statement of that kind. I think the swing can be answered. The question is, who is going to do it?

I want to tell you briefly what young men in one country are doing. I have just come from Japan. There you have a gigantic explosion of industry. You have people who for generations were hungry, now faced for the first time with the possibility of becoming rich. And you also have a very great feeling about the United States—not always favorable—plus a very strong Communist Party line.

There is in Japan a youth organization called the Seinendan. It has 4,300,000 members. The Communists put in twenty men. America put in millions of dollars. At the end of six months the whole machine was about to be swung into the Communist camp. We got 104 of the Seinendan to come to America. We lived with them night and day for three months. We had to deal with theft and dope. We had to deal, of course, with ordinary adultery—people being blackmailed because they were sleeping with other men's daughters. We had to deal with the problem of men with men.

We got these young Japanese straight. When we got them straight, Communism lost its grip on them. Ikeda, the Prime

Minister, and Kishi, the last Prime Minister, both told me
that had the Seinendan been captured by Communism, Japan
today would be Communist.

The torrential burst of industry in Japan—something
which America experienced one hundred years ago and is still
experiencing—is thrusting young Japanese out into a new
world. They buy machines their parents never knew. They
have money to spend that would have kept their grandfathers
going a year. But they don't know where to go.

Now Masahide Shibusawa, grandson of the founder of
modern industrial Japan and son of the Finance Minister and
Governor of the Bank of Japan, has appealed for 10,000
young Japanese to be trained in Moral Re-Armament before
the Olympics. He knows the plan of China and Russia for the
Olympics is to demonstrate to the world's young athletes who
go to Tokyo, a Japanese youth communized. Russia and
China want them all to be given the Communist Party line.

Here is a letter from Shibusawa. He is writing about young
university men and women, many of them formerly of the
extreme Left or Right, who have enlisted with him in a greater
revolution. Writing about this force and the play they have
written, Shibusawa says:

"They are going to Hokkaido, the Northern Island.
All the Generals—the Chief Commandant of the Army
and Commanders of Divisions—are eager to have the
student force on this island. They say they must have
an answer quickly to disintegration. They want us to
leave Tokyo on January 25. They are assigning an Air
Force plane to fly us north from Tokyo. This will save
time and money. They are planning every detail, lending us white winter fur coats, giving us special freezing
weather food rations.

"They are planning a six weeks' campaign to cover the whole island. Every place we go they want us to impact the soldiers and the civilian community as well. The heads of banks, military leaders, heads of the youth department and professors of the University of Hokkaido are jointly considering sending 300 youth every month to Odawara for ten days' training in Moral Re-Armament from April to July. That will create a thousand trained young men from Hokkaido. They are planning further, using this thousand to staff a massive youth training camp in Hokkaido this summer.

"Chiba, Kudo, Sogo and Fujii came for breakfast this morning. [Chiba is head of the Security Committee of the Japanese Diet; Kudo is the president of one of the largest banks; Sogo is head of the National Railways; Fujii is head of the Electric Power Commission.] They pledged to fight in the front line for the youth of their nation. The idea of massive youth training is catching attention everywhere. The press is enthusiastic. One newspaper man says: 'This may be the only way to create a foundation of common thinking for Japan. Then we can save Asia.' "

I want to tell you one more story, and it comes from Italy. The Italians asked a force of Latin American students who had been changed and enlisted—by these Japanese, mark you—to go to Italy. They were there nine months. I heard three days ago from one of the great European Cardinals. He wrote that the nine months spent by these South American students in southern Italy had produced a force in every town and village visited which was not only fighting for Moral Re-Armament, but multiplying. He told me that the reason southern Italy—the most heavily Communized part of the country—did not increase its Communist vote in the last election was because of the work we had done there. He now wants us to go to the north.

A new play of mine called "Through the Garden Wall" has just opened in Rome. It had a successful run in London. Here is what the Communist and anti-Communist press said about it in yesterday's papers in Rome. *L'Unità,* the national Communist daily, wrote: "Howard, famous in his own country for successful literary works, is conscious of the need for a revolution that renews everything, though from the Christian perspective. He is conscious of the need to suppress divisions that split humanity into blocs and keep the world on the edge of atomic catastrophe. Howard wants a discussion. He wants a change. Bridges are better than blocs. This moral, social commitment is mirrored in his plays."

That is the Communist newspaper. If you think I am a Communist, you are wrong. I am not. What I want to do is capture the world for a far bigger concept than Communism, and in my experience you don't do it by shouting at them: "Damn you, you're Communist. We're against you." This sort of thing exercises your lungs. It accomplishes precisely nothing. Except that you get a pat on the back from certain elements in America.

"From the far Left to the far Right (I am reading you a cable) Rome's press greeted the premiere of your play with the liveliest interest. *Il Popolo,* organ of the Christian Democratic Party, and *L'Unità,* the Communist paper, both agreed the basic theme of the play represents the wall between two worlds, a wall made up of mistrust, suspicion and hate."

Il Popolo, the Christian Democrat paper, wrote: "The theme is good, so is the aim." *L'Unità* commented: "It was a genuine success. There are elements of interest that are by no means of a cheap popular appeal—and moments of delicate psychology."

I am not saying this to boost my play. What I am saying is, cannot we get governments in the free world to make an intelligent attempt to win the whole world to something new? Or have we got to go on in fear, perpetuating the divisions that are bound to destroy us all?

Lord Beaverbrook wrote to me three days ago and one sentence from his letter was: "Opposition is your best gift." Well, all I can say is, we are thankful for our gifts! But, ladies and gentlemen, may I tell you this: Some say I am pacifist, bless their hearts! If being a "pacifist" means that I love peace and will pursue it, of course it is true. Any sane person wants peace. But if they mean that I will not stand up and be counted in a fight against tyranny, they are wrong!

If they think a man like me would give his life to something Nazi, or anti-Semitic, or anti-labor, or anti-black, or anti-white, or anti-capitalist, or anti-Communist, they are crazy. My life is given to humanity. And I may tell you in this modern age it is the only intelligent use of a human life. Unless some of us grip this task and carry the thought forward fifty years, the clock is going to stop.

4

*"I wish men of great intellectual
stature would give as much attention
to character as they give to the
new frontiers of discovery.
You do not get people spending
as much intelligent thought and
sweat on the development of man's
character and ability to live with
his brother man, as on developing
his wealth, his power and his
scientific knowledge."*

Revolution of Character

The Center for the Study of
Democratic Institutions,
Santa Barbara, California
December 26, 1963

IT IS A VERY GREAT PRIVILEGE to be invited to meet with you gentlemen this morning. I suffer under many disadvantages, not the least of them being that when I was younger I played games with considerable enthusiasm, and men of intellect know that sportsmen are all bone from ear to ear. Therefore it is with a certain humility, and at the same time very real pleasure, that I accept the invitation to talk to men like yourselves.

Plainly, in this kind of discussion, you cannot attempt either to cover the whole field, or indeed, to justify some of the things you say in terms of proof. You have to assume certain common ground. And the common ground I am going to assume is, first, that all of us believe liberty is, at least, desirable. Second, we believe that atomic war is not the best solution to an explosion of population; that the division on the earth between East and West, so-called, is possibly not so urgent as the division between fat and thin, between rich and poor, between people of certain intellectual and social privileges and people without those privileges;

and, also, that with mankind as it is, we face either a calamity possibly greater than anything mankind has yet known, or alternatively, an age of enlightenment such as history has not yet reached.

Now in my lifetime—I am 55—two world wars have come out of the heart of what used to be called the Christian West. Fascism has come out of the West. Hitlerism has come out of the West. Enormous economic degradation in my country, in the midst of the possibilities of great plenty, has come out of the West. We also have allowed the frustrations of color, class, social division and injustice to reach a point where these provide the rationale, the motif, of world Communism.

On the other hand, you have the Communist world where there have been monumental social and economic developments. But you have Mr. Khrushchev only a few months ago saying publicly in Moscow that after forty-six years of socialist experiment, they have failed to create the new type of man which he believes necessary to make socialism work. He is looking for "a new type of man." That is his phrase, not mine.

You also have a division between China and Russia. Frankly I do not rejoice in it. I want to see some vast group of men creating a form of society that *works*. Obviously, from the power politics point of view, there can be an immediate advantage for free men in this split in the Communist bloc. But in terms of the future of humanity, I do not rejoice. I hope that men will discover, somehow, how to live together.

I wish men of great intellectual stature would give as much attention to character as they give to the new frontiers of discovery that push human knowledge beyond the bounds where most people can understand it—and sometimes I think beyond the bounds where these men themselves understand it. You do not get people in the modern world spending as much intelligent care and thought and sweat on the development of man's character and ability to live with his brother man, as on developing his wealth, his power and his scientific knowledge.

I would like to tell you two or three stories of what is actually happening in the world. We had 72 Japanese students with us in India. They came for the most part from Waseda University. Students of Waseda organized the riots that kept President Eisenhower out of Japan. When Robert Kennedy first went to speak there they shouted him down. From that same University came the right-wing students who organized the public assassination by sword of the leader of the Socialist Party when he was addressing a meeting some months ago. You have the extreme Right; you have the extreme Left; and you have students who are violent, frightened, embittered, and at the same time, highly intelligent.

They asked me to talk there and I went. People said I would be shouted down. Well, for one reason or another I was not. I chose as my subject the theme, "Beyond Communism to Revolution." I said that Communism might, in terms of social and economic injustice, be an arm that people felt could achieve aims for their country, for their color, for their class; but that in terms of an atomic age, it was a bow and arrow mentality—that the theory of the class struggle, carried to its logical conclusion, must result in atomic war between two great power groups.

I happened to have met two ambassadors from Communist countries who had recently talked with Chou En-lai and Mao Tse-tung. Chou En-lai had told them categorically that he felt war was not only inevitable but necessary for the triumph of Communism. His calculation was that three hundred million people would be destroyed in the process.

I said to the students: "If you are going to adopt the Communist line as your weapon in that kind of world, you are living in the Middle Ages. You are outmoded. We have got to have a revolutionary concept which includes the whole of humanity; which aims to put right the massive economic and social differences between men, but also aims to teach men to go forward into the next stage of human evolution, where they learn to live together."

Khrushchev, as you know, has got that problem right now in Russia. I don't want to go into it further, but I can give you chapter and verse.

These Japanese students took this so seriously that they began to apply the principles of change in their own lives. They saw that hate was a sign of immaturity in the modern age. That was a considerable step, because most of them had been brought up with the concept of the class struggle as their natural weapon. They began to deal with hate as it existed in their family circles and in their university. They wrote a play which they took to the great student centers of Japan.

At this moment in Quebec, Canada, there is a large group of Latin American students. They are putting on a play which they wrote called "El Condor." This play gives the answer to the passionate anti-Americanism that is now bedeviling the lives of so many in Latin America. I am not here to defend the United States, for you men can do that better than I can. But anyone today who grows up with hate against another nation actually grows up warped. His brain may grow, but it grows in the wrong direction. He develops a twist.

We had a conference in Miami, and a man called Bethlem came to it. He had twice been the Ambassador of Brazil to other countries. He saw at the conference a play called "The Ladder." After the final curtain he said: "The central figure in that drama is myself."

Now Bethlem is tough. He is a general and an industrialist as well as a diplomat. He is not a sentimentalist nor a religious man. He was there with his wife on their way to New York. The idea of the play had such a profound effect on him that he turned and went back to Brazil. He called a meeting of some of the leading industrialists in his country.

He talked to these men about the gap between words and actions. He talked about the power and influence they held and the selfishness that actually possessed them. They were intelligent men, living selfishly while trying to teach a nation how to live. That was his theme. He took very simple points. He said: "We employ men. We urge them to be honest. But we cheat on our taxes." He said: "We in Latin America make a great point of chastity for our wives, but you all know we ourselves are not chaste. I for my part am going to stop that."

General Bethlem had such an effect on the students of Latin America that a number of them not only changed but decided they wanted to join with him in bringing a new concept of character, aim and motive to other people.

Marshal Tavora, one of the great military figures of Brazil and a man of complete integrity, later told Pope John: "The work of Moral Re-Armament has saved my country from civil war." That was his assessment.

These Latin American students have not only gone through their own countries with their play, but they have spent nine months in the South of Italy, in the poorest quarters, giving their convictions to the people there. Last week I had a letter from a friend in Rome who had just seen two cardinals. They both told him that the effect these Brazilians and Peruvians had had in Italy was still growing in the villages and towns six months after they left.

They have now gone up to Quebec. What will happen up there, I don't know. But when my friend here, Dr. Campbell, was there two weeks ago and tried to get into the theatre where their play was being shown, he could not get tickets. Finally, when they forced the door open to get Dr. Campbell in, four people were forced out by the crowd inside. That was the measure of the audiences they were getting, and of the public response.

Two personal experiences in dealing with convinced Communists might interest you. The first is one of analysis and diagnosis; the second, what you can do to a militant revolutionary if you have a bigger revolutionary concept.

In India, on Finnish Independence Day a few weeks ago, the Finnish Ambassador, who knows our work, invited me to celebrate with him. All the Diplomatic Corps were there. It was at just the time when Chou En-lai had applied to be allowed to over-fly India on his way to Africa, and Mr. Nehru had not yet said "yes" or "no."

There was a Chinese diplomat at this party, a man about my age. I noticed he was quite by himself in a corner, with the crowds milling about and the Indians rather shy of talking to him. I went up and introduced myself. We started talking. He knew all about our work. It is interesting, by the way, that the Communist world understands what we are doing. It understands what we are doing far better, as a matter of fact, than do well-meaning, pious and sometimes small people in the free world. This Chinese said to me: "You've got a play running in Delhi now called 'Space Is So Startling.'"

I said: "Yes." He asked what it was about. I told him. He laughed, and started talking about the Christians in China.

I said to him: "You had them there for a long time." He said: "Yes, and now they have gone." I asked: "What happened?" He replied: "They were intensely interested in people's souls. And they were very interested in filling their churches. But we were interested in the nation. We had a plan for the nation. That's why we won China." That was his assessment. He added: "I don't have any faith at all. Personal salvation may be a very good thing, but if you have a revolutionary concept for a nation or a continent, you are bound to win out over people who are interested only in a human soul or filling a church."

It struck me as a point which all men of faith in the free world, and especially all Christians, should at least weigh. It was a frank statement from the Chinese Communist angle.

In Washington, the last time I was there, I was invited to the Liberian Embassy. They do things well there and in terms of hospitality it is probably one of the finest embassies in Washington. I got there on time because I had another appointment soon after. The only other person not a Liberian when I arrived was a very alert, intelligent-looking, active individual who was systematically talking to every single African in the place. I heard afterward that he was regarded as the most successful Communizer in Washington. He was the First Secretary of the Russian Embassy.

He came up to me, thinking I was a British diplomat, which I suppose some people would take as a compliment. He said: "Do you know Switzerland?" I replied: "Yes." He asked: "Do you know the people engaged in the atomic disarmament talks there?" I said: "Yes." Then he said: "Of course we in the Soviets have one great advantage over you people in the West." I asked: "What is it?" He answered:

"We have a very strong ideology, out to change the world, and you have a very weak ideology." This was his language, not mine. I asked: "Do we in the West have an ideology at all?" He roared with laughter. He said: "Oh, no, you have no ideology in the West. You have none at all."

At that moment the Ambassador of Ethiopia came up. He happened to know me and flung his arms in the air and said: "Why, Peter, what are you doing in Washington? And how is Moral Re-Armament getting along?" The Russian registered very strongly at this point. As soon as the Ethiopian had left, he turned to me and said: "Moral Re-Armament—you are against us." Just like that. I replied: "I would not put it like that at all." He asked: "What is your attitude?" I answered: "Well, we just think you are out of date, that's all. You are outmoded." He took rather a dim view of this and started attacking me quite briskly. He said: "Human nature cannot be changed." I said: "Human nature can be changed. I have seen it change." So he asked me to give him examples.

I told him about a key incident in the freeing of Morocco. A French settler, whose contact with MRA had transformed his attitude of superiority toward the Moroccans, called his workers together and said, "I have a wine cellar. For me it is an indulgence. To you, as Moslems, it is an offense. Will you help me destroy the wine cellar?" They did.

A leading Moroccan Nationalist who heard this true tale, was so impressed that he himself changed and gave up his hatred of the French. His bitter enemy was El Glaoui, Pasha of Marrakesh, whose actions had led to the exile of the Sultan by the French. The Nationalist apologized to El Glaoui for his hatred. The Pasha was moved to tears. Within a week the impossible happened. El Glaoui prostrated himself before the Sultan and asked his forgiveness.

Shortly afterward the Sultan was able to return to his

country. He became King Mohammed V. Later France gave Morocco her liberty and the land was saved from bloodshed.

The Russian said to me: "If you can change human nature, I shall have to rethink all my theory." He said it lightly. "Well," I said, "you can."

A girl came up with a tray and offered us smokes. I declined. The Russian took a cigarette and urged me: "Go on, smoke! Is there a rule against smoking in Moral Re-Armament?" I answered: "No, there is no rule against smoking in Moral Re-Armament." He asked: "Why won't you smoke then?" I replied: "My life is dedicated to revolution. I wouldn't think of wasting one cent of my money on tobacco." He was astonished. He said: "Does it mean as much to you as that?" I answered: "Why the hell do you Communists think you are the only men in the world who will sacrifice for what you believe?" It was quite a fresh thought to him because he had lived some time in the free world.

Then we went into the garden. He was growing angry by now. There was a long table. He said: "Come on, let's have a drink. They won't charge you for a drink here." So I took a Coke. He again turned on me with some savagery: "Go on, is there a rule in Moral Re-Armament against drinking?" I said: "No, there is no rule against drinking." He asked: "Why won't you drink, then?" I replied: "When I'm with a man like you, I prefer to keep my head clear." We laughed. Mind you, that was not the whole story. What I did not tell him was that I know from my own experience, if you are out to change men, but have one habit that has you beaten, you cannot help them in habits that have them beaten.

When we said good-bye, this Russian said to me: "We are going to win." I answered: "I don't think you are." He said: "Come and see me next time you are in Washington."

Men like myself, without the backing of government,

without backing from the authorities, with a great deal of misunderstanding from people who are fed the wrong things by knaves, and sometimes are glad to hear the wrong things and pass them on like fools—we have to do this work of dealing with the nature of men. We have to do it at a time when, unless this problem is solved, unless human nature is dealt with thoroughly and drastically on a colossal scale, we face the greatest catastrophe of history.

I wish governments, men of power, men of influence, men of great intellectual ability, would undertake that task. I think it is the essential task, but it is the one thing people will not undertake. The snag about it is that if you do undertake it, it means you have to start with yourself, because there is nobody more reactionary than the man in the modern world who is determined to see the world different but absolutely refuses to be different himself. That is the heart of the matter.

In terms of belief, we have to deal first with the people who say they believe in God. They are a dwindling number. To make my own position clear, I do believe in God. I have come to this belief from a position of rational atheism because of an experience in my own life and of seeing things happen around me. But that is not the point I want to talk about this morning.

Most people who say they believe in God have presented an image to the world of a faith that is largely concerned either with their personal comfort, or with maintaining the status quo and keeping other people satisfied with the social and economic injustice which it suits such men to maintain. Of course, if God were like that, God deserves to get the treatment in the modern world He is getting.

If we could get the men of God actually to become the most passionate revolutionaries in the modern world and to live together as people ought to live who believe in God,

I do not think there would be the slightest threat to liberty. If the men who still believe in God learned to make God the most revolutionary force in their lives and in the lives of their communities, the whole world would say: "Of course, that's how we are meant to live." That is part of our battle. It is a very hard part of our battle, because if you tackle the righteous, they get far more angry than anyone else, and they start talking to you about theology and all kinds of things.

We also have to deal with people who quite sincerely have no faith or belief in God. With men like that we are entitled to suggest that they face the experimental challenge of absolute moral standards. For we cannot get humanity straight if men are resolutely determined to maintain their own selfish attitudes. That should be clear to anybody.

It is also clear to me that mere economic change, mere change in environment, does not in itself produce a revolutionary answer to selfishness quickly enough to meet the challenge of our times. I have found in dealing with both Communists and anti-Communists in Europe, America, Latin America and Asia, that when they are willing to accept the challenge of absolute moral standards—honesty, purity, unselfishness and love—and get straight on basic points like that in their own lives, they are prone to see the nation straighter.

I am amazed at the number of people who intensely deplore *color* prejudice but have a very strong *class* prejudice, up or down. These attitudes seem to me equally immature and equally dangerous. But some people see no connection between the two.

In my own country when I was a boy, if you went to the right school or had the right background or the right education, on the whole you looked down on people who didn't. And of course there is still some of that prejudice in Britain, as you all know. Nowadays it seems to me equally fallacious that, if you come from a working-class background and work your way upwards by scholarships to become the new intellectuals, the new intelligentsia, you should look down on everybody else. This seems to me equally divisive, and equally a threat to democracy.

Senator Fulbright, who has done a great deal in this world, comes out strongly against moral absolutism and says he thinks it is a great threat to democracy. He even went so far as to say that it was the moral absolutism—or relics of it— in American life that led to the assassination of President Kennedy. I don't want to say much about that except that it is a flight of thinking which certainly leaves me spellbound —rather like saying that at the opening of the hunting season in America, so many people get shot because Americans are such good marksmen. It seems to me the real reason was not moral absolutism, but the lack of it.

I am not talking about the Gestapo mentality that pries into other men's lives. I am dead against that. Nor am I talking about the moral relativism which says: "I am perfect. You are imperfect. Damn you and we will persecute you." I *am* talking about absolute love which says: "All of us have something of the right spirit in us. We must all of us help one another to change until that right spirit becomes dominant in our lives, and we are willing to be revolutionary enough to apply the test to ourselves first."

In the chaotic, dangerous and immensely exciting world we are living in today, democracy is not meant to be a free-for-all at any price. Democracy depends on the inner discipline and the standards of conduct that free men choose to adopt if they are going to stay free.

5

*"You fight the Communists
economically. You fight them
politically. You fight them militarily
if you must. But where is the
common ideology shared by all
free men which says to the
Communist world: 'You are out of
date; you are outmoded. We are
going to put this world right
far quicker than you can do it'?"*

Three Prongs, or Four

"Dellwood,"
Mount Kisco, New York
January 26, 1964

A SHORT TIME AGO I was in Berlin. It is a grim place. The wall is just about as high as the walls here. If you stop and look over it, the guards stop and look at you. They have guns. And you move on because they are not looking at you to see what you're like.

They are men under orders.

The suffering of that hideous act of cruelty is not confined to one side of the wall. On both sides people suffer and endure. And the invisible walls we create in our free society are just as cruel.

I think of the massive barriers we British have built between ourselves and the rest of the world through our conceit, our vanity, and our pride. I think we have somewhat changed, but our attitude has caused a lot of trouble and is still creating bloodshed in certain parts of the world. I think of the childishness of disliking someone else because he happens to be born of a different color. We are like children— only children don't do this.

A friend of mine in Oxford, a very brilliant man, wrote to Radio Moscow recently and asked if they would broadcast on whether the Russians thought they could change human nature. He didn't expect to get a reply, but, lo and behold, Radio Moscow gave a full-length broadcast on the subject. They said: "Of course, you can change human nature. We're doing it. We have 600,000 of our best youth in Siberia. They are breaking new ground. They are making new towns. It's true that thousands of them come back, but thousands of them stay. You may say it is like the Americans when they opened up the West. The difference is that the Americans went seeking El Dorado. Our youth seek no wealth, because they know they are not going to get it. They are engaged in creating new towns, new cities, new agriculture, a new civilization for the Soviets. We can actually create men and women who will sacrifice without personal gain for the sake of the community."

I think Communism is hellishly wrong. It is anti-God. Its world aim is to control and change the whole character of human society. I am not a Communist. I never have been a Communist. I never will be a Communist. But unless we face the challenge that in the Communist camp they are actually creating a spirit of discipline and sacrifice, enforced if you like, but not wholly enforced—unless we match our life against that challenge, we shall lose our freedom. Before God, this is the issue which faces America today—young and old, rich and poor.

I was talking the other day to a very powerful and very fine American. I do not say those things with the slightest cynicism. He was a fine American, and an honorable man. We got to talking about Vietnam. He became very angry and said: "Huh, the Vietnamese are just natives living in a swamp. They don't know anything about democracy." Now I cannot speak for America. But I'm bound to tell you that I know a lot of Vietnamese who are far more highly educated than many people living in my country. They have high-grade Parisian degrees. They are highly intelligent people. It is perfectly true that the man working in the paddy fields in Vietnam knows about as much educationally as my friends working on the farms of England. They are farm workers. Thank God that we still have millions of them left. But educated Vietnamese are highly intelligent and trained people. To this American they were remote, just "natives living in a swamp."

What about that attitude in America? Now Diem is dead. All over Asia the Buddhists know how he died. It is a story not yet told in America. It is a horrible tale, whether you agree with the man's policies or not.

There was a man called Hitler. He used to say about people of different color, or the Jews: "Huh, they don't count. They are just inferior beings. Let them die." There was a man called Stalin. He said: "Huh, the people living on the land, let two million of them starve. They are not important. Let them go."

What is the difference in those attitudes—in the mind of God? That is the thing you have got to face in the United States of America. Are you going to build a land sex-centered, money-minded, self-absorbed, or are you going to build a country where people stand for the right as God gives them to see it? If you can go that last way, America will win the world.

My country depends on you. The way America goes, the world will go. And unless we can face this materialism, this putting of things first—women, men, money, place, power, recognition, anything—before God, we create the breeding ground of Hitlerism and Stalinism and the deathbed of freedom. If we get that straight, we will have the greatest revolution of this century. That is the challenge to America.

The Camelback Inn, Phoenix, Arizona
February 16, 1964

Now I MUST MAKE CLEAR where I stand on Communism, because many people talk about Communism, and Communism is a fact that history has to reckon with.

I think Communism is the greatest threat to the future liberty of man that has ever appeared on the earth. I think it is the spirit of anti-Christ, organized with the massive power of great states. I think it is anti-God, anti-freedom, and I think it must be answered. The question is *how* to answer it.

Now you can answer it by submission. Personally, I am one of those who will never submit. Some people in my country say: "Better Red than dead." I say: "Better dead than yellow." I do not think free men should in any circumstances whatsoever consent to losing their liberty for the sake of a peace that may not last anyway, and submit to a tyranny that in my view is far more dangerous and far-reaching than anything Fascism ever created.

Then you can make war. And it may come to war. But in modern war remember that in twenty-four hours the great cities of the United States, all the great cities of my country and the great cities of Russia and other parts of Europe will be devastated. It is a colossal decision and a colossal price to pay. Politically speaking, I wonder what president of any country, if he had that stark choice, would say "yes"—so that for the sake of Berlin, or some other distant city, that button is pressed. It is easy to talk about it. It is harder to ponder what you or I would do if we were in that lonely and terrible position of power.

The third way of answering it is to out-revolutionize Communism. Now don't get excited when I say "out-revolutionize Communism." I believe that any Christian should be far more revolutionary than any Communist. I come from a Christian country. At least, we call ourselves Christian. Supposing Khrushchev had the use of the largest buildings in every great city in my country, in every village in my country, a very large and highly skilled, fully paid full-time staff of agents, and a captive audience once a week. Where do you think my country would be at the end of two or three months? The whole climate would have changed.

I do not think that America as a gigantic do-gooder, or as a gigantic one-worlder, is very effective. You have given the whole world the impression that you want everybody on earth not only to like America but to be like America. You may not stand for one world, but the world thinks you do. And it is an image that needs very rapidly and intelligently to be dissolved if you are to out-revolutionize in Asia, in Africa, in Latin America and in Europe the titanic bid of Communism to capture the heart of humanity.

You fight the Communists economically. You fight them politically. You fight them militarily if you must. But where is the common ideology shared by all free men which says to the Communist world: "You are out of date; you are outmoded. We are going to put this world right far quicker than you can do it. Come and help us. But you must change if you do. We are not going to take you on your present terms"?

I am not such a fool as to think that Chou En-lai, Mao Tse-tung and Khrushchev would throw their hats in the air.

I do know from experience that millions of people behind the Iron Curtain and millions more in Asia and Africa and Latin America would turn resolutely to the free world's camp if we offered them a revolutionary alternative to Communism. But you cannot fight a four-pronged battle with only three prongs. America and my country, Heaven knows, desperately need an idea in our heads and an answer in our hearts as well as a bomb and a dollar in our hands if freedom is to survive.

Unless your country and mine choose to be governed by God, we may condemn millions of others in Africa and Asia and elsewhere to be ruled by tyrants. And choosing to be governed by God does not just mean a formal church attendance, important as that is. It does not just mean saying I am a good fellow and I wish everybody were like me. It means accepting a passion, a philosophy, a plan, a discipline to establish what is right in family life, in industrial life, in American life and in the life of the modern world.

Why not an American nation where everybody learns to lead the world into the paths of freedom and peace?

6

"We do not expect enough from women. Women have not only the intelligence, but above all the heart power, to heal the hates of the modern world. Unless somebody undertakes that task, man is surely going to destroy himself with the problems he has created."

Heart Power and Hate Power

To the Women of Los Angeles,
Ambassador Hotel,
February 5, and the
Women of New York,
Waldorf-Astoria,
March 3, 1964

THANK YOU for your gracious hospitality. I would like to ask my wife to speak to you for a moment. I owe a great deal to her. She is Greek. Her uncle was General Metaxas, Prime Minister of Greece, who during the war when the enemy invaded his country said the one word: "No." She has something that she and I would like you to hear before I speak.

MRS. PETER HOWARD:
I want to apologize from the bottom of my heart to you Americans for what is happening on Cyprus. I feel it very deeply that you are being turned away when you have given of your lives, your treasure and your heart to us. As a Greek I want to tell you that I certainly am going to fight for my country to change.

This morning I was thinking what would have happened on Cyprus if we could have had five women in the last year who understood how to change, how to change

63

others, and how to reach the thousands on the island and give them an answer to hate and to bitterness. That is the work we women must do all over the world now, because the world is sliding fast and we've got to learn to cure these things in people's hearts. You and I can do it. I certainly want to give the rest of my life to doing these things for people, on this side of the Iron Curtain and the other side.

We do not expect enough from women. We expect them to bring us into the world. So far none of us has arrived on this planet without their help. We expect them to nurse us when we are preparing to depart from here. In between times, we expect them to provide color of hats, hair and garments, with painted eyelashes, lips, cheeks and other appendages for our delight—if such things do indeed delight us. We expect them to bring comfort to our bedrooms, beauty to our living rooms and the right number of calories suitably disguised to our dining tables.

But, frankly, most men have the same attitude towards women as the English are believed to have towards those who are not English. They say on the continent of Europe that you can tell an Englishman anywhere—but you cannot tell him much. Nowadays women might, with justice, say that you can tell a man anywhere, or almost anywhere, but you cannot tell him much. Women are braver than men. As a rule they have more guts. They need them because they have to live with men.

In the world today men have fostered the theory that women are glorious, expensive, sometimes lovable toys. If you have enough money, you can look after them fabulously well. Most of them give the best they have got, but do not expect women to play a decisive part in modern history.

Women have not only the intelligence, but above all the heart power, to heal the hates of the modern world. Unless somebody undertakes that task, man is surely going to destroy himself with the problems he has created.

There was an old gentleman who used to be the Prime Minister of my country. He was called Benjamin Disraeli. Later he became Lord Beaconsfield. He had a marvelous wife, some years older than himself. When he came back late at night from the House of Commons into that house on Curzon Street, his wife used to go to every window lighting candles, so that at two o'clock or three o'clock or four o'clock in the morning as he returned home, that whole house would be ablaze. Once when he was going down to make his budget speech the door of the cab, unknown to him, crushed her hand. She got out of the cab, went with him into Parliament, where old "Dizzy" made a tremendous speech. She never said one word to him, although her hand was crushed and bleeding.

There is still a quality in womanhood, particularly in American womanhood, that can grapple with the divisions of our time—divisions of color, of class, of race or background which threaten to destroy us. Unless women care enough to do that, I am not sure that the men are going to do it. Because so far we've not made a very good show.

Disraeli was once caught up in a mighty debate. The question was whether man is beast or spirit, ape or angel. Disraeli went down to Oxford, my old university, and he said: "Gentlemen, if it is a choice between apes and angels, I am on the side of the angels." That does not mean that any of us are angels. Perhaps you are. I am not. But seriously, is man an animal or is he a spirit? Is there any difference between women and monkeys except lipstick, jewelry and furs? If there is no difference, if there is nothing in our hearts except animal matter, then we have no criticism and no answer whatsoever to the technique of slaughterhouse and zoo. We can say nothing to the filthy paraphernalia of Fascism that in my lifetime has torn a world apart. We can say nothing to the callous and cruel indifference of Communism that in my lifetime has not only divided the world, but threatens to engulf it.

But if there is something in the heart of every man, woman and child which makes us different from a cow, a rhinoceros or a barnyard fowl, it is time we started to live in such a way that an observer coming to earth would recognize the difference.

Nowadays there are moral codes invented by senior people for the children, the teenagers, the up-and-comers. A first-rate American teenager in a big college said to me the other day: "The grown-ups talk about moral codes. It's hooey." I said: "Why hooey?" He said: "We see the way they live. What's the point of getting home by midnight if you find your parents half drunk when you get there?"

All that you and I accept as decent in life is under savage attack. What are the Russian cosmonauts doing? They are running all through Africa. The lady cosmonaut is seeing the Queen of my country. And what is their message? "We have been up there. We have been around. There is no God. It is all for the birds."

I will read you exactly what they say on Radio Moscow: "Our rocket has bypassed the moon. We have not discovered God. We have turned lights out in heaven that no man will be able to put on again. We are breaking the yoke of the gospel, the opiate of the masses. Let us go forth and Christ shall be relegated to mythology." That is not a Christian message. It is a hard-boiled political message by extremely realistic revolutionaries, who know what they are out for in the world. The people today in the free world who talk about God, who go to church—and I wish everybody did—and who live as if He did not exist, in their board rooms, in their bedrooms, in their family circles, do more to further the cause of Communism than most ardent Communists. That is the thing we must face if we are honest.

In Italy now there is a play of mine running. It is called "Through the Garden Wall." It had a successful run in London at the Westminster Theatre. It ran for nine months. Pina Renzi, one of the top actresses in Italy, is playing the lead in that play. It is having big box-office triumphs. The Communist trade unions bought the house out in Rome and sent their men to it across the country. It is a play that challenges Communists frontally on how men get changed without a change in environment. It is not against a change in environment—it is a revolutionary play about how you can actually change without necessarily having environment changed first.

God comes in in the third act. The Communists in Rome last month were talking to a friend of mine who happens to be a trade-union official. They said: "God has come in through the back door of the Communist headquarters. It is unfair."

Now I want to tell you the kind of thing we endure in terms of sheer silly smear. Moral Re-Armament stands frontally against materialism. If you stand against materialism in the name of God, people don't always tell the truth about you. I don't blame them. I understand it. But don't swallow all the things you hear. In this play of mine the hero happens to be Jewish, a man called Dr. Gold—and Dr. Gold, of course, does well in the play. One of the Arab ambassadors, who will be nameless, came to see it in London. This man circularized all the other Arab embassies in London saying: "Howard is a dangerous Zionist. Don't go to his play." Actually I knew a good many Arab ambassadors and most of them came to see what Howard was doing. So it suited us fine.

When I got to Hollywood a good friend of mine said to me: "Ah ha! I am told you are an anti-Semitic Christian." Well, that's fine. I take that too, though it does not happen to be true. But here is the cream of it. The Catholic press and the Communist press have given this play high reviews in Rome. The Communist paper says: "Anybody can recognize in Dr. Gold the character of the late Pope John." So there you are!

The scuttlebutt we get doesn't worry me a bit. What people say about me doesn't matter a rind of cheese. What does matter is that intelligent forces in your country and mine are determined to see Communism capture the world. They know that so long as Moral Re-Armament is expanding this cannot happen. Of course they smear us, but what disturbs me is that fools of integrity swallow the lies invented by intelligent knaves. That does trouble me.

The heart power of the women of America could shift the policies of the modern world. America's strength is her heart power. Her weakness is her hate power. I will admit to you women something which few men admit. You actually get the men you want in this and every nation.

We are as pure in our ways and motives as the women wish us to be, neither more nor less.

America's strength, if the women so decide, will be as the strength of ten because her heart and life are pure. I am not interested just in personal, private habits. But I believe that if men take public office in your country or mine, they should live straight. Nobody is forced to run for anything. Everybody has free choice. But if you or I wish to run for congressman, senator or for any public office, our private life at once becomes a public matter. We must have public men in our countries who are daylight honest and straight. I am not interested in a sort of prodnosery of puritanism. I hate it. I don't like that snide prodding and prying.

A friend of mine, a surgeon, is about to go to Africa with a force to try and save Africa from Communism. He is Dr. Close. He is a good surgeon. He was in the Congo at the time the disaster struck when the Belgians were pushed out by world opinion. Do you know that the only surgeon in the Congo for months was that American? I salute him. He tells me that in his training for three years every day he was told how to wash his hands. It is important if you are going to do surgery that you know how to wash your hands so they are perfectly clean. Half an hour every day—how to wash your hands. But washing your hands isn't surgery.

We are engaged in a monumental job of world surgery. Peking knows it. Moscow knows it. I wish to high heaven the democracies would understand we are trying to give them an ideology that will save freedom and secure peace on the earth. I am not giving my life to washing my hands or yours. I have to keep my hands clean. Supposing I had a mistress round the corner? Supposing I had embezzled money? Supposing I was bullyable or bribable? Where would our work go?

We have undertaken this mammoth task of world surgery. We may be able to do it in time. I don't know. Time is running out. We need your help to do it better. If you see ways in which we can do more, please tell us. If you know ways we can get more money, please tell us. We are asked at this moment to send a force to Morocco. We cannot do it. We haven't the money. We are asked to send a force to Cyprus. We cannot do it. We are asked to send a force to Latin America. We cannot do it. We just have to do all we can with what we have got.

But I suggest to you very seriously, consider whether America can win the world unless she plans for the world. Moscow and Peking plan every day for Mr. U.S.A. Mr. and Mrs. U.S.A., are you planning every day to take the whole of humanity forward into a hate-free, greed-free world that is the next step of human evolution? And will Mrs. U.S.A. lead the way?

7

*"What is your plan to build a world
that really works? A world where
no man goes hungry, where
everybody has a decent home to live
in, and the chance for an education
to give him a full life.
If this young generation undertook
that task, the whole of history
would shift."*

Tomorrow's American

University of Southern California,
Los Angeles
January 8, 1964

WE HAVE BEEN HAVING a most interesting lunch. I felt as if I were back at my University of Oxford doing my philosophy classes. My sympathy is with all those people who have their final examinations next week.

There was a marvelous theory put forward at lunch, that if you have anything "goody-goody," you must have something "baddy-baddy." In other words, if anybody dares to mention the name of God, which nowadays takes increasing courage in the free world, you must have somebody stand up and blaspheme. I wonder what in the world that philosophy would do if it were applied to the food we eat. If you have a good shrimp, you've got to eat a bad shrimp. If you have an omelet made of good eggs, you must have one made of bad eggs. I think those people who, in the name of liberty, propagate a philosophy which says that everything good must be balanced by an argument for something bad, should try it on their food. We'll send them the bad doctor first instead of the good doctor. However, that's just a philosophical comment.

Nowadays cynicism has become a great virtue. If you have

a belief in the spirit of man, if you have a belief in Almighty God, if you have a belief in sound family life, if you have a belief in chastity, you are regarded as a kind of "square" and an "old fogey." Well, I must plead to being an "old fogey" and a "square" because I do believe in all those things. I am not cynical.

I believe that if America fails to accept the challenge of history, the world will fail. But I also believe America is not going to fail.

Together we have got to create men free from hate, fear and selfishness—a type of man as different from the Dollar-and-Sex man as a Spaceman is from a man pushing a wheelbarrow. That is our task. And make no mistake. If primitive man had not discovered the wheel, sophisticated men would not today be wheeling through space, and contemplating the colonization of the stars.

We need a revolution to carry the whole world forward fast to its next stage of human evolution—to outpace the growth of human power, wealth and skill with a growth in human character. If we succeed, we shall secure the peace and build a new world. We cannot do one without the other.

There is nothing more futile, in my opinion, than those who talk passionately about peace and believe in peace and long for peace, but at the same time refuse to pay the price of building a new world fit for every man, woman and child to live in. We've got to undertake that supreme task together. If we fail, we shall enter a new dark age, or rather a new Red age—or we shall see man destroy himself with his own skill and power and the problems he has created.

This revolution is one which all civilized people, certainly all people of faith, are called upon to undertake together.

It is the most fascinating, most difficult and most demanding task of modern times.

Merely to abuse people for being wrong, while at the same time hoping to continue to live undisturbed, is reactionary and selfish. We've got to usher in a revolution big enough to change all men, Communist and anti-Communist, and enlist all men in the tasks of God for continent after continent.

I want to tell you about two young men, one of them named Gandhi and the other Shibusawa. I am looking in America for the young men and young women who are going to match what they are doing by taking up the monumental challenge that now faces American youth.

In India there is Rajmohan Gandhi, the grandson of Mahatma Gandhi. He is 28 years of age. He faces a very grave situation in his country with widespread corruption, massive failure to pay income tax, bribery of government officials and mounting friction between government and business. He is also faced with the Chinese coming in over the northern border.

Gandhi has marched from the south of India, right through the great cities, to Delhi. Everywhere he has gone he has held mass meetings. He has said to the students of his country: "It's no good asking for honest administration in Delhi if you are dishonest in your exams. It's no good asking for unity in the nation, if your families are divided. If we want a new India, we have got to create a new pattern in Indian youth."

He has had an overwhelming response. The men in command of the Indian Army, Navy and Air Force have asked him and his friends to go to every military camp in the country, to talk to the young recruits who may have to lay down their lives for India. They come into the Armed Forces without an aim. They are not fit. They don't know where they are going. They are purposeless. Somebody has got to give them a direction for their lives and a love for their country. They have asked Gandhi to do it.

Mr. Nehru, in Cabinet two or three weeks ago, was told by some of his fellow ministers that Gandhi wants to replace him as the Prime Minister of India. This does not happen to be true, but it is a sign of what this young man of 28 has already accomplished in the public conscience, and in the mass flow of a great nation.

India is on the brink. She needs armed strength. She needs dollar aid. The whole world owes its freedom to America's generosity and strength. I thank God on my knees night and morning for the strength and might of this country. But dollars and guns alone will never do it.

Someone has got to deal with the lack of character, the lack of aim in Asia, in Europe, in Latin America, and even in America. If the young generation doesn't do it, it is we older ones who must admit we have failed.

Then I take you to Burma, which we passed through on our way to Japan. They have a military administration there. All the universities and colleges are closed. Many of the students have taken to the hills. I was told that when the students in Rangoon rioted, they picked up 202 bodies after the police had stopped firing. Not quite the same as California! But they are the same kind of people. They have their families. They have their hopes. They have their dreams.

In that situation, I was informed, the spirit of Moral Re-Armament has never been so strong as it is today. They told me: "The people in the villages and towns at last realize that without a moral and spiritual change, without a new motive, our country is going into a slavery such as we have never experienced before, and from which we may never escape."

In Japan, there is Masahide Shibusawa, 33 years of age. His great-grandfather was the pioneer of modern industrial Japan. His father was Governor of the Bank of Japan and Finance Minister.

By the time of the Olympics, Shibusawa wants 10,000 Japanese youth trained in Moral Re-Armament. He wants to show the youth of the world that something is rising in Japan that is new—not the old Fascist tendencies, not the new militant Red tendencies, but youth that not only love freedom, but are willing to pay the price of it by discipline in their own lives. The government is backing him. Trade-union leaders are backing him. Universities are backing him. The military are backing him to the point where they are flying his force all round Japan, and feeding and clothing them as they go.

I want to talk to you for a moment about freedom. It seems to me there are two immaturities at large in the world today. One is the immaturity of hate. America's strength is her heart power. No nation in the whole of history has done what this nation has done for nations like mine. As long as men can think and read, your generosity and courage will be recorded. But your weakness is your hate power.

Supposing America could really become, in the next five years, a country absolutely free of hate. Supposing this campus became absolutely free of hate—in families, between students, between faculty and students—would you have something to say to the modern world? You'd have something to say that the United Nations have never yet said.

You'd have something to say that the United Kingdom has never yet said. You'd have something to say that the U.S.S.R. has never yet said. And frankly, you'd have something to say that the U.S.A. has never yet said. But the whole world is waiting for it to be said.

The world is full of idealists who poison the atmosphere around them with hatred of somebody else because of their color, their race, their poverty, their wealth or background. They are part of the problem, whether they know it or not.

The other great immaturity is that of self-expression. It takes the form of doing what I like, when I like, regardless of what happens to my neighbor. Some people call it freedom. It is actually the inevitable death of freedom. It creates a belief that I'm basically a good chap, that my country is basically the best country, and that if only others understood what a good chap I am, and what a fine country mine is, everything would be in order. It is so soft, it is so stupid, but year after year millions of our dollars are squandered in the worship of this false idol.

I first came across Moral Re-Armament as a columnist who was paid one of the highest salaries in my country for my exposés and investigations. I was cynical—I had no faith at all. I had spent three years studying philosophy at Oxford. It had the effect of giving me a very sharp brain which I used to kill my conscience. That is how I emerged from Oxford. It also taught me how to earn a living, which I did very successfully. It was a partial education, not a whole education.

I went along to investigate Moral Re-Armament and I straightaway found people who were adopting the most intelligent attitude to modern events I had ever seen. They said any idea that keeps anybody out is too divisive and too dangerous for the times we live in. Therefore, if you're going to get everybody *in,* everybody has got to change. And if you want to see history change, the most practical place to start is with yourself and your own nation.

Then they talked to me about absolute moral standards. When they started talking about purity and honesty and unselfishness and love, it didn't take long for an Oxford philosopher to prove they were wrong. I instantly said: "Well, of course, all standards of behavior are relative." And a coal miner, well trained in Marxism, said something I never forgot. He said: "If you have a standard at all, it must be absolute. Otherwise it is no standard." I got angry because I knew it was true. And in one simple sentence years of philosophic training were swept aside. I was confronted with reality.

Then I asked: "What do you really think?" They said: "We think that people without faith can start with absolute moral standards. That's the experimental method. Spend a few minutes facing absolute moral standards and see where you would have to begin if you really wanted to remake the world. We believe that God has a plan for every man, woman and child in the world, and if you have faith, if you listen to Him, He'll tell you where to start." I said: "Don't give me that stuff, because I don't believe in God." They said: "That's fine. If you don't believe in God, you wouldn't mind making the experiment of listening to Him, would you?"

I could not object to that, although it made me feel squeamish. I said, "Thank you very much," and went away. London had a heavy air-raid that night. I had certain duties to perform and was out all night. When I got home in the morning I thought: "Look here, this is either rubbish, or it's the most important thing you ever heard in your life. Have you got guts enough to try it?"

We British are very proud, and if anybody suggests we are too proud to make an honest experiment of that kind, sheer pride makes us try it. So I tried. Pride can be useful at times. I got very simple ideas about honesty in the home. I had always wanted my children to be honest with me—my sons and my daughter—but I had never been honest with them. I had always wanted our government to be honest, but I wasn't honest about taxes. Quite simple things!

I longed to see a world truly united, but I only had one brother and I was jealous of him. I felt my parents liked him better than they liked me. Absolutely childish! There was I, a grown man, probably the most feared commentator in the country, jealous of my only brother. I had the idea that I ought to write and put it right. Do you know, three times I went down to that mail box in Fleet Street, with a letter. Three times when I got there I tore it up. I said: "No!" In the end I wrote that letter.

I tell this somewhat personal story to show you the amazing things that happen if you obey the ideas you get. My brother came to see me. He was, of course, in the Army, fighting. He gave me hell. He said: "I've always thought that about you. Now I know it's true." And he left. And I felt: "Well, there's not much in this." Two hours later he came back again, and he said: "Let's talk." We talked for the first time in years as brothers are meant to talk, with no shadows between us. We went to see my mother and father next day. The rift in our family was mended. That boy—because he was only a boy to me—found the beginnings of a faith in God. He was killed at Arnhem. And I had nearly been too proud to do the simple thing that helped him. Give him advice, sure! Give him money, yes! Give him a job, yes! Pat him on the back and say he is a great fellow, yes! But not do the one thing that actually helped him find a meaning and purpose for his life.

America is the most wealthy, powerful nation of our time, or of any time in human history. There has never been a nation so wealthy and powerful. But I don't think America understands the world she lives in. I don't think she understands Communism, and I don't think she possesses the answer to it. I think she is against it. That's a different story. I believe America thinks Communism is the sharing of wealth and that free enterprise is the reply. Now, don't get me wrong. I am all for free enterprise, but it has little appeal to thin men who possess nothing. Have you ever thought of that? If you are an Asian or an African, with too little to eat, and no hope of getting much tomorrow, talk of free enterprise has no great appeal.

In any case, Communism is far more than making thin men fat, or fat men thin. And that is about the level at which some people put it in this country. Communism is a bid to alter the character of humanity. It is a ruthless determination to achieve that end, defiantly demonstrating that man is nothing but water, chemicals, gas and dust, assembled by accident, conditioned by environment and dispersed into oblivion as the brief light of day fades and night falls.

Communism is the worship of materialism—the worship of rubles or dollars, the worship of human flesh and human brain, the worship of success or recognition, the worship of heroes whether they are dressed up as dictators or presidents. It is putting man first. Communism is the denial of God. It condones the immorality that springs, and springs only, from a disbelief in Him.

The answer to Communism is not merely anti-Communism. Hitler was the greatest anti-Communist that ever lived.

Have you ever thought of that? He succeeded in spreading Communism across half the globe and killing himself in the process.

Men who speak against Communism, but have hatred in their hearts against members of their own family, their fellow students, or members of the faculty, against people of another class, race or color, are in fact spreading the Communism they denounce and deny. A free-for-all society, money-minded, sex-centered, success-driven, may strengthen but will never answer Stalinism or Hitlerism.

One nation God-centered—or if you don't believe in God, a nation centered on the morality and spirit and character of men—teaching men to accept absolute values of honesty, purity, unselfishness and love, and to obey that inner voice which distinguishes all men from any beast. Such a nation will lead mankind forward beyond known frontiers into the new territory of lasting human freedom. I believe our task is to bind up the wounds of centuries and set all continents free. And with all my heart I believe the youth of America can do it.

[*Mr. Howard received many other requests to speak to youth audiences throughout the country. Following are extracts from a few of these addresses.*]

Manhattanville College, Purchase, New York
January 28, 1964

I WOULD LIKE TO TALK TO YOU for a moment about revolution, because I am a revolutionary. My life is dedicated to the purpose of remaking and revolutionizing the entire world. I want something new for Communist and non-Communist, for black and white, for everybody on earth.

I believe myself that in India and in Asia and in my country and even perhaps in America, we have got to create a new generation of people who actually live straight and who pay the price in their own lives of getting their nations straight.

I have noticed in Britain that if you mention purity nowadays to younger people, a lot of them start smiling and laughing. I remember the words of a wise friend of mine named Canon Streeter, who was the head of Queen's College, Oxford, and he always said about laughter: "Laughter is the shout of delight with which a fool recognizes himself."

I am an old man of fifty-five. I have children whom I love and two grandchildren. I tell you this. Unless we, who have some faith, can accept the fact that God who gave us our physique can teach us how to control it, we are lost. We are lost because we present to the faithless a picture of people living a faith in such a way that it has no effect on our lives. So we sell them short.

What is needed is a revolutionary American; an American who is more revolutionary, with a deeper sense of urgency and destiny for every man and every country he or she goes into, than any Communist; an American committed to a far more fundamental and radical revolution than any revolutionary of materialism. We have got to create a new generation of people who actually live free from fear, free from the great drives that we know in our hearts are wrong, but which we submit to because it makes us popular.

I was talking about a month ago to some of the cleverest men in America, men so much cleverer than I am that I often just did not understand what they were talking about. They work in one of those places where you have a huge placard put on you and a man walks with you all the time to see you don't steal the secrets. They raised this point with me: "Is MRA Utopian?" At the end of an hour they were quite sure we weren't, because as a matter of fact we knew a great deal more about what was going on in the world than they did— and, furthermore, we were dealing with it.

Then I said to them: "Now, what are your aims?" The chairman, a very nice man, said to me: "In the long run we think we're losing the war"—a somber thing to hear from an American in his position. He said: "We have stockholders. We are paying them handsome dividends. We have multiplied our industry, and when an election comes along we give $5,000 to the Democrats and $5,000 to the Republicans." Of course, he meant that they kept a foot in both camps according to who was elected.

I said: "You are the most unreal men I ever met. You have the face to tell me with your knowledge that you are losing the war, yet all you are living for is putting money in your stockholders' pockets and paying an equal sum to both parties. It's utterly Utopian." The chairman had the grace to say, if you'll forgive it: "My God, he's right."

We must never get the idea that it is Utopian to deal with human nature. The truth is that it is Utopian to think you can put the world right *without* dealing with human nature.

Youth Forum
"Dellwood," Mt. Kisco, New York
March 7, 1964

THERE IS A PHRASE which you may or may not have heard of: "Look back in anger." It was the story of a play, a book, an attitude toward life.

I look forward in revolt. I am in deep, passionate and

determined revolt against things as they are in the modern world. One thing I hate like poison is that a generation, my own generation, has created a terrible problem in the world for you to inherit, and then blames you for living in a way we don't like. I think it is dead wrong.

I am in revolt against a world where man technologically and industrially can create enough for everybody's need, but where in Asia you have millions of families living on a total annual income of less than $350 a year. I hate it. If you go to the south of India, you sit on the ground in their huts. All they have to eat in a family is a double handful of heaped rice. That is their day's ration, with perhaps a bit of fish if they are lucky enough to have caught it. They share it with you.

Now that sort of thing need not go on. We've got to stop it.

If I had my choice of being born at any time in human history, I would choose to be born just about the time you all were born. If I had a second choice, I would choose the time I was born. And I intend to live as long as I possibly can, because, in spite of the difficulties, this is the most adventurous, fascinating, exciting time in the whole long history of man.

I want to tell you in a few minutes some of the things that are being done. You cannot expect, you know, in twenty minutes to cover the whole story of Moral Re-Armament in the modern world. Radio Moscow described our work in a world broadcast as "a global ideology with bridgeheads on every continent, which is in its final phase of total expansion throughout the world. It has the power to capture radical, revolutionary minds."

At the heart of British public life today a young man has arisen who happens to have married my daughter, and who is having a profound effect on the thinking of my country. His name is Patrick Wolrige-Gordon. He is 28 years old. He was the youngest member of the British House of Commons.

He decided that he was going to put a revolution at the heart of his personal and political life. He decided to put right what was wrong socially, politically, economically.

He represents a constituency which is almost feudal. It is East Aberdeenshire in Scotland. The lairds there—the people of privilege and power—still pretty well run the show. What they say goes. Three of them sent for my son-in-law and said: "Wolrige-Gordon, we don't like this stand. It affects our way of life. You will please withdraw from Parliament. We want you to take the gentleman's way out." Wolrige-Gordon replied: "I was elected by the people. I am answerable to the people. When the people tell me to go, I will go. Until then, I stay."

He went to the hospital for an operation. The men who did not want him called a meeting of the party executive board. By 19 votes to 16, with 32 abstentions, they kicked Wolrige-Gordon out. The press got hold of the story. There is one thing about the British—we are very slow to perceive things, but if we perceive injustice, for some reason we still dislike it. Thank God! And the whole national press began to write about this. Wolrige-Gordon demanded as a right a meeting of the association, which is all the people in the constituency interested in his party. For three months, almost every day, it was front-page news throughout Britain.

The meeting of the association came. Most of Wolrige-Gordon's constituents are farmers or fishermen. I regard them as the salt of the earth. They swarmed into that place. My daughter, Anne, was taken in by the fishermen and taken right up front. When men raised an attack on Moral Re-Armament and what Wolrige-Gordon stood for, my daughter, who inherits her mother's courage, stood up in the front, pointed a finger at them and said, "It's a lie!" and sat down again. That was her only contribution.

That crowd, by an overwhelming majority, threw out the whole executive board. They elected a new executive. A very well-known leader of public life told me just before I left home that Wolrige-Gordon and his wife had actually succeeded, by the moral stand they took, in shifting the thinking of a large section of the Establishment in Britain, who are the people who run the country.

The most active propagandists in the modern world are those who, if you don't drink, or dope, or sleep with people, or do as they do, try and push their ways down your throat and call you a "square" if you refuse. I am not going to be told what to do by that kind of person. My life is my own and nobody is going to tell me that I've got to do the thing that in my heart I feel is wrong. I want people to stand straight and say: "I am going to do what in my heart I believe to be right and if the popular thing is wrong, I prefer to be unpopular rather than compromise." That was the basis on which this country was built, incidentally. If certain people had not believed that, there would have been no free United States.

But there's also another side to all this. I understand nowadays people argue that there may be no such thing as right and wrong, that everybody does what he wants, that "nobody is going to tell me anything." All right. But if you say that to yourself, you have nothing whatever to say to a Hitler or a Stalin.

Hitler and Stalin chose that course. They decided that what suited them was right. If I decide what is right for me and to hell with everybody else, how can I point a finger at any dictator? How can I point a finger at Stalin, who says, "Two million people can be killed because the State needs it," when I say, "If a child's unwanted, let's kill it. Let's have an abortion"? How can I say a word to Hitler, who decides to lacerate, mutilate and torture people who happen to be born Jewish, if in my own life I say, "I'm going to do what I think suits me best, and that is my idea of right and wrong"? Hitler would reply: "That is precisely what I say."

I have read in *Time* magazine that cover story about the "mores" of America. It says that America seems to be a sex-sodden society. It says in effect that the only yardstick of behavior between the sexes nowadays is whether people get hurt.

Now I want to put to you younger people seriously: Who got hurt when my generation decided to live just as we chose? You did. What did you inherit? What are you going to hand on to your children? A boy and a girl take up together. It ends up perhaps with bed. Then one of them wants to break. Who gets hurt?

By 1970 there will be on present statistics ten million illegitimate children in the United States. Now, anybody who blames a child for being illegitimate is foolish. It is no more a child's fault than it is the fault of that tree for growing there. But ten million illegitimate children growing up with that particular hardship that society still imposes—who gets hurt? Those two heedless people; or that child, who has a life to live? Also, it is possible our countries may get hurt.

The destruction of the last world war need never have taken place if a few of my generation had taken real responsibility for putting the world right. We always wanted someone else to change, but we would never change. Absolute moral standards—not for us. Therefore we compromised and compromised and compromised and then were astonished to find other nations taking no hope from us and themselves compromising. And in the end it cost our blood. In the end it cost us a generation. It cost us wealth. It cost us in my country a lot of our human comfort.

Churchill said something which I think is still true about the situation we face in the world right now: "If you will not fight for the right when you can easily win without bloodshed, if you will not fight when your victory can be sure, you may come to a moment when you have to fight, with all the odds against you and only a precarious chance to survive. There may even be a worse case. You may have to fight when there is no hope of victory, and it would be better to perish than live in slavery."

That is the challenge facing us. I think it is desperately late, but not too late. And we at Mackinac Island, Michigan, this year are going to try and match the 10,000 young Indians Gandhi is training in Moral Re-Armament, the 10,000 young Japanese Shibusawa is training in Moral Re-Armament, the 10,000 British that are following the leadership given by men like Wolrige-Gordon. We believe here in America you have got the quality of youth to take on the task of remaking the world.

Williams College
Williamstown, Massachusetts
March 5, 1964

IT IS A PLEASURE TO ME to be with you. I only had the privilege of going to the second finest seat of learning in the

modern world, and we have just had a meal such as we were
never given when I was at Oxford.

I believe that there is going to be a revolutionary change
and advance in human society. In Latin America today two-
thirds of the total population is under 25 years of age. By
1966 you will have fully half the population of the United
States under 25. The future of the world depends on where
that young and rising generation takes humanity. The future
of the world depends on whether you know where you are
going and love what you know. When I was young, we mostly
had no idea what we were living for, except ourselves. And
you have reaped the harvest of it.

My generation reaped slavery, torture, death, war, because
we were indifferent to everything happening in the world
around us except our own careers. I don't want your generation to reap that same bitter harvest.

My generation at Oxford had a funny outlook. Aldous
Huxley was one of our great heroes. We were absolutely
determined that nobody should tell us what to do. But we
used our brains to tell our conscience and our heart that what
we wanted was all right. We succeeded.

And then some of us did something even more far-reaching. We got important jobs and used our Oxford-trained
intelligence to kill the conscience of the nation in order to
make the nation more comfortable for us to live in. I think
that was pretty good dictatorship. But of course we did it in
the name of liberty.

Then Huxley grew older. This is what he said some years
later in *Ends and Means:*

"I had motives for not wanting the world to have a
meaning, consequently assumed that it had none and

was able without any difficulty to find satisfying reasons
for this assumption. For myself, as no doubt for most
of my contemporaries, the philosophy of meaningless-
ness was essentially a matter of liberation. The liberation we desired was simultaneously a liberation from a
certain kind of political and economic system and liberation from a certain system of morality. We objected
to the morality because it interfered with our sexual
freedom."

That is a very honest statement.

J. D. Unwin wrote a book called *Sex and Culture* which
Huxley in his heyday praised as a very great book and which
is still accepted as a classic on this particular theme. Unwin
writes:

> "Sometimes a man has been heard to declare that he
> wishes both to enjoy the advantages of high culture and
> to abolish continence. Any human society is free to
> choose either to display great energy or to enjoy sexual
> license. The evidence is that it cannot do both for more
> than one generation."

I believe very simply that we are going to see a colossal
swing in the customs, ways and economies of modern life.
I believe that the intangibles have become the imperatives,
because neither education, nor environment, nor law, important as all these things are, can actually deal with the hate in
human hearts, the selfishness that allows some men to walk
around the earth far too fat, while millions walk around far
too thin, the sheer indifference that builds those unseen
barriers between man and man, nation and nation, class and
class, race and race.

Those things have got to be dealt with. And those who declare they cannot be dealt with condemn this world to destruction, because sooner or later people are going to think it suits their side to try and destroy the other side. Then you are taking the world headlong into the calamity Karl Marx predicted as the ultimate end of the class war. I think Karl Marx was and is wrong. But we have got to prove him wrong by demonstrating, as people of free will under God, that we can choose to live in a way that assures freedom for our children.

Everybody ought to be allowed freedom to choose. It is no good trying to keep God out of schools and colleges if you allow anti-God freedom in those same schools and colleges. It is contrary to liberty. And I think every one of us has something in our hearts, something in our spirits which makes us different from pigs wearing clothes or furs and jewels and lipstick. I think there is that something in every man, woman and child on earth which enables him to make a choice between right and wrong. I think if free men exercise that choice and make it regnant in free society, we shall have a society with "mores" so compelling that the whole world says: "That is the way men are meant to live."

Youth Forum
Los Angeles, California
February 7, 1964

LET ME TELL YOU what I believe. You have got the leadership of this country in your hands, whether you want it or not. It's a colossal responsibility.

Every single day people in Peking and Moscow are planning for you. They want to take over this country. They're not wicked people. They're people with an idea they believe is right. What is your plan for the masses of China, for the masses of Russia, for Asia, Africa, the entire world? What is your plan to build a world that really works? A world absolutely free from prejudice. A world where no man goes hungry so long as anybody has something to give him. A world where everybody has a decent home to live in. A world where everyone has the chance for an education to give him a full life. Now, is that true Americanism? Is that true revolution? Is it worth doing?

I believe truly that if this young generation undertook that task, and let the world know it had undertaken it, the whole of history would shift. I believe if we shrink from that task, the whole world may be destroyed. And I do not accept the notion that young Americans today are so soft, so selfish, so small that they will refuse the biggest challenge.

My generation has talked big and lived small. I believe your generation can talk big and live bigger.

8

*"The different races in America are
her strength and glory. They can
be her supersonic missile of
revolution in the modern world.
I do not say, 'Be patient.'
I say, 'Be passionate for something
far bigger than color.'"*

What Color Is God's Skin?

Wheat Street Baptist Church,
Atlanta, Georgia
February 23, 1964

ONE HUNDRED YEARS AGO and more, President Lincoln signed his proclamation of emancipation. It was a revolutionary aim. Today our aim is more revolutionary and more far-reaching in fulfilment. It is a revolution for every red-blooded American. And I must remind you that every American's blood is red. It is and ever will be the greatest revolution of all time whereby the Cross of Christ will transform the modern world.

Some people are afraid of the word "revolution." No man of faith should be. "Thy kingdom come. Thy Will be done on earth as it is in Heaven." If that phrase becomes no longer a pious drone but a passionate commitment, it is more revolutionary than any Fascist state or than anything Karl Marx concocted. It affects all we say, do, think and are. It involves race, class, color, personality and nationhood.

In new patterns of power unfolding across every continent, revolution to change the aim and character of humanity is blazing in urgency. Let us ensure that blaze creates more light and less heat. Otherwise the world may be lost in darkness. Man with his mind has wrenched secrets from earth and atom that can in this generation give all men everywhere food to eat, homes wherein to dwell, a fair chance and proper background in life. He has with his skill plunged like Leviathan beneath arctic ice caps and ridden with Mercury among the stars. Man's hands control strength to populate new planets or to destroy this one with the problems he has created. His heart still lingers in the dust and debris of senile, sterile prejudice, outworn attitudes, pride and selfishness that have crumbled and failed.

Too many still walk the earth who are too fat, too many who are far too thin. There is enough for everyone's need, but not for everyone's greed. But man does not yet care enough and share enough so everybody has enough. At a time when it is God's will and man's desiring for everybody—black, brown, white, yellow and red—to walk with head upheld in dignity, equality and peace, selfishness alone breaks homes, divides races, multiplies hate, bedevils the hope of a moral maturity to match the technological and industrial opportunity of our times.

The different races in America are her strength and glory. They can be her supersonic missile of revolution in the modern world. They are no handicap. They are an asset that no other country possesses.

In my lifetime, whole countries have been taken over by the cruel dictatorship of Fascism and countless millions are now controlled by the godless philosophy of Communism. To our shame, not one city, not one state, can boast that it is controlled by the living God.

Supposing America, with her Negro and Latin American and Caucasian and Indian minorities, were able to proclaim in honesty to the listening earth: "Come and see how all men everywhere are meant to live. We need you all in our bid to change world history which is the destiny of our age. In this dangerous, essential task, black men, white men, all men are needed. Here in this land we live like sons and daughters of the God who created all men equal, planting in each human heart the knowledge of right and wrong that makes man different from a beast."

Africa, emerging into freedom, would leap with joy and clasp hands across the ocean. Asia would turn her eyes to the West. Latin America would forget the flirtation of Fidel Castro and follow the advances of her comrade in the North.

This brings me to a question no man can answer. What color is God's skin?

Laws are important. Laws are essential. I am one who believes that legislation must often march or even run ahead of the growth in man's character which makes much legislation unnecessary. But laws cannot by themselves alter the character of a human heart.

On the day President Kennedy was assassinated, I talked with two American Negroes. They spoke of civil rights. They agreed that a civil rights bill with teeth would probably pass through Congress. Then one said: "Whatever laws pass Congress, I can never trust a white man. It is in my bones to hate them all." Unless you have been a white man, you don't know what it means to have that said to you.

Englishmen like myself were taught from our mothers' knees to believe that because we were white and English we were better than everybody else. It breeds the immaturity of that effortless superiority, often unconscious, always so cruel, that millions across the face of the earth have experienced and resented. We do not look down on people because they have a different colored skin. We just feel nicely sorry for all those who are not born English.

I told those American Negroes how I, an ordinary English-man, had made the experiment of listening to the voice of God, the inner voice that speaks to each human heart. I had seen that it was the selfishness, arrogance and pride of men like myself which had caused untold misery, suffering and injustice.

When I spoke to the men and women of the Mau-Mau, detained in the Athi River Camp in Kenya, they covered their faces as I drew near. They would not look at a white man. My first words were: "I was born white. I could not help it, could I?" They began to look at me. It began to slide upon their understanding that it was as immature and ignorant to hate a man because he was born white, as to hate him because he was born black, brilliant, foolish, ugly, beautiful, big, small, Jew or Arab. When I had finished speaking, their leaders came to me and said: "We were educated in Christian schools. We lost our faith and became cynical of everything except violence to achieve liberty, because of the way we saw white Christians live. We want you to know that if we had dreamed white men could speak and think as we heard you speak today, there would have been no Mau-Mau in Kenya."

> When I survey the wondrous Cross
>   On which the Prince of Glory died,
> My richest gain I count but loss
>   And pour contempt on all my pride.

I felt in my heart the shame and agony of the words these Kenyans spoke to me. I wept. Some of these former Mau-Mau leaders have become my friends. They saw white men change. They learned that black men, too, could change. They changed. They now are on the march with people of all colors and races to bring God's revolution to the continent of Africa. They understand that violence, sometimes regarded as a good servant, can swiftly become a bad master, and that history never long remains on the side of hate. Hate knows no color bar. Neither does love. Heart-power is America's strength. Hate-power is her weakness.

The two American Negroes said to me: "Do you think education and environment can change human nature?" I long for every man, woman and child to have the best education and environment civilization can provide, but neither environment nor education changed me. God did. My wife, not English, but married to me for thirty-one years, says: "Moral Re-Armament changes everybody—even the English. And if that can happen, there's hope for the whole world."

Everybody wants to see the other fellow, the other class, the other race, the other nation change. Everybody is waiting for the other to begin. Modern Fascists and reactionaries are those who want things different but are unwilling to be different themselves. Modern pioneers and revolutionaries are those who are so impatient with things as they are, so passionate for things as they must be, that they pay the price in their own lives of the change they wish to see in others. A hate-filled man will never unite a society or even a family. Men driven by greed, pride or fear will never build justice, liberty or lasting peace.

The white man's world is ebbing. For a long time the white man has been in a minority on the face of the earth. By accident of history, by design of power, white men have controlled much of the planet. That time is swiftly ending. Communications, education, automation—all will combine to shift the power balance of humanity.

God made men in different colors. A white man's world, in the sense that a white man, because of the color of his skin, is closer to God than is his neighbor, affronts the will of the Almighty and the understanding and conscience of humanity. So does a black man's world. So does a world of yellow or red domination. We need a world where all men walk the earth with the dignity of brotherhood that should be normal to all who accept the fatherhood of God.

The Negro is neither worse nor better than his neighbor. The same is true of the white man. We all have our loftier side, and our more debased. There are two sides to each coin —heads and tails. In the West there has been too much tail, too little head. And the heart, which could and should be the leaven of society, lies forgotten between pride of intellect and lust of desire. We exploit our wife or somebody else's wife, our neighbor, our business rival, and scream out against exploitation.

America will set the continents free when she experiences lasting freedom in her own heart—freedom from the immaturity of hate, the under-development of selfishness, and the infantility of impurity and dirt.

I number many Africans among my friends. Not long ago, I traveled with some of them in this country. It is strange that in communities where the white American will no longer listen to the Negro, and the Negro will no longer listen to the white American, both will heed the voice of Africa. These Africans were invited to the homes of Southerners, white and black. Some of them, people of prominence and distinction in their own countries, stayed in the homes of American Negroes. At the end of a few days, they came to me and said: "Some of them treat us in the same way that they say some white men treat them. The same superiority, the same condescension, the same contempt."

We white men are prone to tell everybody else how to live and what to do. But we are too proud to listen to the voice of God, and ourselves, in obedience, learn how to live. We preach unity with passion and call ourselves the United Kingdom or the United States. We transfer idealism to the United Nations but we remain, behind the doors of our homes, our offices, our churches, deeply divided from each other—by jealousy, ambition, greed or prejudice. I pray the black man does not fall into the white man's ways in this regard.

Today, the long-awaited tide of history flows towards the non-white races. Those tides will lift burdens of the centuries and wipe out bloodstains in the sands of time. Be sure that tide elevates all humanity. You cannot expect every Negro, any more than you can expect every white man, to be a genius of ability, a paragon of virtue, a miracle of grace. But I hope, pray and expect that the Negro people of the United States will have the wisdom, understanding and human greatness to avoid mistakes that men like myself have made before them.

There was once a great Baptist preacher called Spurgeon. Multitudes came to sit at his feet. One day he said: "We Baptists can proudly make our boast. We never persecuted those who differed from us on religious grounds." When the "Amens" and "Hallelujahs" died away, Spurgeon added: "We never had the chance."

The black man's chance is surely coming. What will he do with it? I do not say: "Be patient." I say: "Be passionate for something far bigger than color. Be passionate for an answer big enough to include everybody, powerful enough to change everybody, fundamental enough to satisfy the longings for bread, work and the hope of a new world that lie in the heart of the teeming millions of the earth."

Segregation yesterday. Confrontation today. Transformation tomorrow. Let the hands of the black man stretch out above the heads of governments and nationalities to embrace and welcome all people who are ready with them to remake the modern world.

Unless we accept a world aim, we may be lost in narrow disputations. It is difficult, if not impossible, for others to place confidence in a system of democracy that preaches inalienable rights of the individual with its lips, but robs men of their rights with its customs. Yet it is true that nothing would suit the enemies of freedom and of America more than to see this country tear itself apart with its internal wars, preoccupying itself with mutual strife, while dictatorship takes over the rest of the world. Some demagogues, enemies of liberty, white and black, inside and outside America, desire to push the problem for the sake of personal power instead of curing it for the sake of all the people.

It is a paradox of our times that Communism, which says it believes only in materialism, bids powerfully for the mind and spirit of humanity. Democracy, which declares its faith that man has the spirit of God, the Holy Spirit within him, bids for the allegiance of humanity with materialistic aid, but without a revolutionary aim for the whole world.

Lenin said: "Our revolution will never succeed until the myth of God is removed from the mind of man." In free society we print on our money, "In God We Trust." But if in truth we place the claims of cash, comfort and color before God, we justify with our lives the theories of Marx no matter what we say with our lips.

It remains my firm belief that crossless Christians have done, and still do, more to camouflage from humanity the reality of Christ's revolution than any Communist or Fascist.

There are sincere men in the free world who have no faith in God. To them it can be said: "Then accept the challenge of living in the way you would wish to see your neighbor live." Absolute moral standards of honesty, purity, unselfishness and love are a yardstick by which all men can measure their conduct and see where change is needed. If you have a standard at all, it must be absolute. Otherwise, it is no standard. And those four standards may prove a ladder that leads a man towards faith.

We say God is love. It is fair to add that throughout history, many who professed a faith in God have hated their neighbor. My wife gave me one of the best definitions of love I have ever known. When first I accepted the challenge of this revolution, I went to her and was as honest with her as I had always wished our children to be with us. She said to me: "Peter, I think I am meant to love you as you are, but to fight for you to become the man you are meant to be."

This I believe is true love, where black loves white, white loves black, all Americans love America, and America loves the modern world enough to live so that black, white and the whole of this torn and suffering earth become as they are meant to be in the mind of the Almighty.

My faith is in modern America. I believe Americans will arise and shine forth with a character that convicts, captivates and changes nation after nation. I believe that those who have suffered most will show the greatest passion and compassion for long-suffering humanity. I believe that those who have been victims of the worst discrimination will be the first to heal the hates and fears of others because they themselves are free from fear and hate. I am convinced that men and women who for generations have drunk the water of tears and eaten the bread of bitterness, will give living water and the bread of life to millions—trembling, longing, hoping, waiting, praying, for the new type of man and the new type of society that will lead the world into lasting justice, liberty and peace.

Those who have passed through the fires of persecution can hold forth one hand to persecutors and persecuted alike, and with the other uplift a flame of freedom to illuminate the earth.

9

"*Is America's revolutionary concept
big enough to include all the
Asians, all the Africans, and the
whole Communist world in the next
step forward in human evolution?
That is Moral Re-Armament.
The labor movement is meant
to understand that, to equip itself
to be a part of it, and then
to help it forward.*"

Labor Can Shift the Nation

Seminar of Officers of Labor Unions
of Southern California, Los Angeles
February 8, 1964

"PEOPLE WHO EXPLOIT or enslave other people forge their own chains." Do you know who said that? You were going to ask me a few questions. I thought I'd ask you one! "People who exploit or enslave other people forge their own chains." Any offers? [Someone in the audience said: "Lincoln."] Well, it ought to be Lincoln, but actually it was Karl Marx, creating the agenda for the First International.

Our work is revolution.

We stand strongly in favor of trade unionism. I wish the whole world were properly united and the workers unionized. I wish the unions themselves were united.

We are utterly opposed to any discrimination of class, color, creed or race. We will fight to the death to bring intelligence to humanity and end all discrimination. We believe in civil rights, but we do not think that legislation goes far enough.

We are out to end the hatred in human hearts created by human arrogance and pride, and to end the human arrogance and pride which creates that hatred. Of course we believe in legislation, of course we believe in laws to make men live as men should live, but we believe that neither environment, education nor laws go far enough in the times we live in. We have got to train men to step forward into a new age where we live together as sane people and as brothers.

I hate poverty. In 1962, according to the figures, one million American farming families lived on less than $1,164 a year. That is terrible. But may I also tell you that many million families in Asia live on a total income of less than $350 a year? I have sat in their huts with them. I have shared their food—a couple of handfuls of rice for the family. They share it with you! If you've gone through that, you've either got to have a heart of steel or you will never forget it. We need that passion for people in our hearts to make us tick.

I rejoice at the prosperity of the American unions. I thank God for the conditions you have achieved. I know the struggle you have had. But I beg you all by the mercy of God, don't forget the people who don't have unions. Don't forget the people who are still oppressed. Don't forget the people who this day as we sit here are going to bed hungry, and waking up tomorrow without hope. If we in the free world forget those people for one instant, the world we create is going to be destroyed.

When I was a boy I went down the Rhondda Valley. I saw some of the finest craftsmen in my country, sitting there year after year without work to do through no fault of their own. They used to say: "Come to have another look at us?" I never forgot it. I'm not sentimental either. I think if we are going to see that there is enough in the world for everybody's need but not for everybody's greed, it means all of us have to participate in a world revolution.

Moral Re-Armament happens to be revolutionary. We challenge every selfish man, whether he's a unionist or an industrialist, black or white. We challenge you to change. Not everybody likes that. We believe that the price of a new world is the decisions made in individual human hearts, starting in our own. A lot of people can tell you about the rugged ill-nature of some steely capitalist, and I know they are selfish! And if you go to the other side of the fence a lot of people can tell you about the bull-headed selfishness of certain union leaders!

We cannot tell you how to do your work. We are not so foolish. Nor, incidentally, do we want to take over your work, as some people say. Of course we are dead against "yellow unions." Of course we're against scabbing. Of course we want to see unions built on a sound level for the sake of America. And we are able sometimes to help.

The textile industry in France had a situation where 600,000 textile workers were under-paid. It happened also to be a situation where management could not pay an increase. This was genuine. Very often it is not. We went to one of the national board of the textile industry, a man named Carmichael. We said to him: "Do you put money before men?" He gave us a powerful talk on the subject of free enterprise. It was wonderful! When he finished we asked: "Do you put profits before people?" He said: "To be honest, I do. I have to. I have to think of my stockholders."

We fought him tooth and nail, because this man called himself a Christian. He changed. He said: "I promise you, from now on I am going to put people before profits." We said: "Right! Will you meet Mercier?" Mercier was Secretary General of the Textile Workers of France, a man who for years had been in the Communist Party. He was absolutely sincere. But he had suffered, and was bitter towards every capitalist. Carmichael said he would meet Mercier.

Mercier came to see him—very cynical. In two and a half hours those two men found agreement. It led finally to a pay increase of 16% for 600,000 workers. The workers responded with a new spirit of productivity in the industry. Every year afterwards the French textile workers received an increase in pay. Mercier, when questioned by the press, said: "Not one cry of hatred, not an hour of work lost, not a drop of blood shed. That is the revolution to which Moral Re-Armament challenges workers and management alike."

Do not believe we can be bought by management. We don't take a cent of salary. We cannot be bullied or bribed. We have only the money that people give us. We have no big "sugar daddies." If anybody wants to bribe us or bully us, let them come and try. We happen to be—with God's help—incorruptible. We all give to this revolution every cent we have in the world.

People talk about my writings. My plays are successful. I heard this morning from Italy that the trade unions have bought out the theatre because they see there is some hope of changing management. That's great. I must also tell you in all honesty that the Catholic press very strongly praises the play because, they say, they think it will bring the unions to a sense of patriotism.

Through my pen I have earned royalties amounting to just over 400,000 pounds sterling since the end of the war. That is well over a million dollars. I give every cent from my books or plays, before they are published, to the work of Moral Re-armament. I do it not from any spirit of nobility. I happen to believe in this work. I wouldn't want to make money out of it. I want you to understand that, because we talk here together sensibly. I may not meet you again. I want you to understand the reality of how we are financed. We are financed by the voluntary sacrifice of hundreds of thousands of people all over the world who pitch in because they care. If you want to see the accounts you can go to Washington and see them. They are audited and filed every year with the U.S. Treasury. There is no mystery.

It is just the same in my country. For the last 25 years in Britain the accounts of Moral Re-Armament have been audited by Price, Waterhouse, filed at Somerset House, and any of you who have a shilling can go and look at them. If you haven't got a shilling come to me when you come to London and I'll give it to you!

I have a farm. Any profits from it go to Moral Re-Armament. The men who work with me know that, they know what I am living for, and they chip in too.

I'd like every capitalist in America to give us large sums of money. They do not. I can think of no better use to which the money could be put. But if you think any capitalist can buy us for the purposes of the right wing you are crazy. We are not for sale. That's one reason why we get attacked—by extreme Right and extreme Left.

It is important that you men understand about American policy in Africa and Latin America because there are in those countries millions and millions of people like ourselves who are attaining freedom and becoming organized, who will affect the future of America. Frankly, American policy in those countries is often blind.

Don't think that every revolutionary who arises today in Africa is a new George Washington. He may be a new Castro or a new Chou En-lai. Be dead sure whom you back.

All our hopes are in America. If America fails, the world fails. But supposing you get the whole Central African bloc Communized and hostile to America. Many trade unions there are associated with the Communist-controlled World Federation of Trade Unions with its headquarters in Prague. This gives the Communists a legitimate ground of operation in these emergent countries. Supposing you get all that section hostile to America. Supposing you get that whole Arab section in the north hostile to Israel. What happens to Israel? Supposing that builds up and America says: "We've got to save Israel." What kind of war are you in? What happens to those African nations is important to the security of America. We in the West don't think. The Communists do.

I give you that picture because sometimes Americans get a wrong steer about countries which are of extreme importance for the future of America.

Cuba is the hard core of Communist revolution in Latin America, the place where it is being planned and carried forward. In the age of atomic power any American President who tried to take his country to war over Cuba would be running colossal hazards and risks. If I were the American President, I'll tell you what I would do. I would give Latin America—Brazil, Mexico, Panama, Chile, Venezuela, Peru, the Argentine—an ideology that actually changes Communists and changes Castroites. I know we can do it because I've seen it happen. I would get a one-way stream of the right ideas flooding into Cuba. Then all those Cubans would arise and say: "This is something we have never had before, this is what we want." You would trim Castro's whiskers. He fought his way into Cuba ideologically. I'd get back into Cuba ideologically.

But in order to do it you need an ideology. It's not done by waving the star-spangled banner and shouting: "Hurrah for free enterprise!" Let me repeat, I do not believe any American President will go to war over Cuba. They dare not. I am not suggesting whether they should or not; I am dealing with reality. I don't think they dare. But Cuba *is* a deadly wound in your flank. And it never need have happened.

We were up in Manaus and Recife in Brazil. Some people in those places go to bed on the muck heaps at night because it's cooler, poor devils! We had 90,000 people in the stadium to hear the evidence and to cheer like thunder on Castro Day. There was a pro-Castro meeting downtown at the same time. Forty-two people came.

Why doesn't America do that? If you did that all over Latin America, you'd have no more trouble with Cuba. The people would say to Castro: "Brother, you're out of date. You've had it." But America doesn't give them an alternative. They don't want to return to the old days when they were exploited—and they're right. They *were* exploited. But they don't actually want Communism. What is America's alternative? You say: "Get rid of Castro and back we'll come." They say: "I'm not sure about that." You've got to fight an ideology with an ideology.

If Moral Re-Armament became the avowed aim and practice of the American State Department, you'd get a response in Latin America you've never had. You would end the corruption in Latin America and get a colossal tide flowing back into Cuba.

I don't think Mr. Khrushchev is in politics for the love of the bright eyes of humanity. One picture in America is that every Communist is a starry idealist who, although slightly mistaken, is someone everybody loves. Khrushchev is a very tough politician. He doesn't want inspection, nor at the moment does he want any relaxation of tension. He's got a line to hold in his own country. He's afraid Israel may get the bomb, as well as France. And he's deadly afraid that by this time next year China will have the bomb, which I think she may. He dare not let his defenses down unless there is a universal letting down of defenses. So he keeps America haggling and baggling. He occasionally gets another chunk off our package. Internally and externally, it suits him to keep this tension going. You are dealing with a very tough "cookie." You will never, never answer an ideological threat without an ideology. It is so simple that even an Englishman can see it. But do you think you can get the Americans to see it? Not on your life!

In Mr. Khrushchev you've got a man who fights you militarily if he has to; he fights you economically all the time; he fights you politically; but above all he has an idea. He drops it into the hearts of people in Cuba. He drops it into the hearts of certain people in America. He drops it into the hearts of millions of people in Latin America, Asia, and Africa.

I would like to meet Khrushchev and Mao Tse-tung; I would like to have a talk with them. That doesn't make me a Communist. Khrushchev wants to win the world for an idea he believes in. I think it is a very narrow and dangerous idea. Any idea in the modern world that keeps anybody out is too small. But Khrushchev does use and exploit the situation we have created. If we are more passionate to cure it than he is to exploit it, I think we will win.

You are the most generous people on God's earth. There has never been anything like American generosity in the whole of human history. You give dollars, you give aid, you send the Peace Corps out to play games with the boys and girls in darkness and light—it's wonderful. You fight if you have to—bravely. Economically yes, politically yes, but where is your ideology?

I wish America could understand that long word "ideology." America thinks that capitalism is the answer to Communism. It's like saying that a dollar bill is the answer to a faith in Buddha. It's a different dimension. It isn't an *answer*. Capitalism is an economic system. Communism is a bid to alter the character of men. It's a wholly different point. But can you get it through the skulls of the British? Very hard! I've got more hope for the Americans. They have more to lose.

Materialism, the worship simply of things, of comfort, of food, of money, of profits, of wages and of nothing more, again and again has proved the deathbed of democracy. I pray Almighty God that American labor understands that it must teach the whole world to live in a new dimension where people are free from selfishness, free from hate, free from fear and free from greed. We want legislation to make that possible. We will fight with you till kingdom come to achieve it. But we will also fight to see that in the ranks of American labor there is such a quality of family life, of union life, of personal life, that the nations say: "If we could live like that crowd—free from prejudice, free from injustice, free from color divisions, free from hate—the whole world would come to maturity." That is our vision for American labor.

Let's be dead sure in your life and in mine that there is no trace of the hatred or bitterness that divides humanity. I'd like every labor leader, every labor leader's wife, to be able to say before God: "I hate no living man. I will not allow any man to drag me so low that I will hate him." That was said by a great American. Just be sure we can say it too.

Let's be sure we understand that the spirit of Moral Re-Armament is the spirit which can make and keep America permanently free.

Moral Re-Armament is what millions of Asians and Africans expect from the free world. They expect far more than dollars—which you so generously give them. They expect a revolutionary concept to live by.

The Communists give them their revolutionary concept. I think it is a very narrow one. It is about 300 years out of date —to blame another class and plan to destroy it by force. But is America's revolutionary concept big enough to include all the Asians, all the Africans, and the whole Communist world in the next step forward in human evolution? That is Moral Re-Armament. Every man inside the labor movement is meant to understand that, to equip himself to be a part of it, and then to help it forward.

Please don't think that anyone here wants to take over the labor movement—we want the labor movement to take on Moral Re-Armament, because it's the one safeguard for America.

I believe that organized American labor can shift America quicker than any other single force. But men like Mr. George Meany, your president, may have as false a picture of Moral Re-Armament as America has of Vietnam. The same people have misled America as have misinformed him, and it is even more dangerous. The leaders of American labor don't need advice from me—I'm not such a prize ass that I think a wandering Englishman can come and tell you American labor men how to organize American labor. But I can tell you what the world demands from America. There is a vacuum, and I can tell you the deadly peril of freedom if that vacuum is not met. We have got to tell the leaders of America the facts and let them decide. But they don't yet have the facts.

Don't think I'm here to make people better. This is an important point because many people think we are a kind of evangelistic concern that comes up and says: "Have you got an itchy pimple? If you'll scratch mine, I'll scratch yours." If you think a man like me would give his life to that, you're nuts! We are in a massive job of world surgery, and the world is a very sick patient. In order to do that job of surgery, we have to clean our hands, but cleaning our hands is not surgery. I am not a bit interested in going around inspecting your hands. I say: "Let's do the surgery together. If we need to clean up, clean up as we go—but let's do the surgery."

Moral Re-Armament exists only insofar as it is lived and applied by people. In terms of people around the world who have been affected by it, the numbers run into scores of millions. That is literally true. It doesn't mean that they're all saints. It does mean that their lives to a greater or less extent have been affected by this work and they are still in touch with it. We never will have a membership because the moment we did that we would become a kind of rival concern to other rival concerns. We don't want to run a rival union; we don't want to run a rival church—or a rival political party. The Republicans need a lot of Moral Re-Armament; and, bluntly, I know Democrats who need a lot of it too.

When I set out as a newspaperman to investigate Moral Re-Armament I found people who were making the most intelligent attempt I had yet seen to answer the contradictions of our age. And I still believe that to be so.

The world is going to be remade—or it is going to be enslaved.

If you can tell us how to do our job better, you will be our friends. We have got to do it better. But as far as we are concerned, we are in there with every drop of our blood, every cent of our money, every ounce of such brains as we have got, till death us do part.

We want to remake the modern world. That is our revolution, and your revolution, and we will carry it through together.

10

"I believe it is our failure in the West to comprehend the nature of this ideological struggle, and to pay the price of winning it, that has put Cuba into the Communist camp. I do not believe we shall recapture Cuba for freedom without either a major war, or an ideological thrust."

Cuba Could Be Free

Everglades Hotel,
Miami, Florida
February 29, 1964

I WAS GRATEFUL for the way the Dean thanked God. It's
called an invocation these days. When I was young it used
to be called grace. Last time I was in the United States with
Dr. Frank Buchman, we had an interesting dinner. We had
with us an atheist. An atheist is somebody who does not believe there's a God and who thinks that the only difference
between us and the pigs is that we have lipstick, furs and nice
suits and spectacles. And like many atheists he was very ag-
gressive. He was a propagandist. All through the meal he
made a strong and vehement case for atheism and godlessness.

Dr. Buchman, who was the host, sat at the end of the table.
He ate his food with enjoyment and seemed not at all put out
by this, but when the meal ended he said: "Well, now, usually
in my house I like to say grace. And I like to say grace at the
end of the meal because then you know what you're thank-
ing God for. But, of course, tonight I've listened to the conversation and I don't particularly want to embarrass any of
my guests. So I tell you what I think we'd better do. We'd

better all sing 'For He's a Jolly Good Fellow'—and we'll all know whom we're singing to."

Now that may seem unorthodox to you, but next day that atheist turned up with his son. There'd been a split in the family. The father felt his boy was a considerable problem. The boy told us that he thought the father might do a little changing too. The man was a plumber by profession. He found a faith and his family was reunited. The bill for plumbing in the house in which Dr. Buchman and all of us were then staying amounted to $1,200. He tore it up. He said: "Of course, I wouldn't think of charging you after what you've given me." So sometimes, when you see people fishing, don't assume because the technique is fresh to you that they're not going to catch fish.

I was interested to hear two mornings ago that a bath had done to that gallant astronaut Glenn what the spheres and galaxies failed to do. He'd sailed through the skies with the greatest of ease, but the poor man slipped on the bathroom floor and it knocked him out. It struck me as very like modern life. We have the capacity to go to new planets. Men, brave men from America, have plunged beneath the Arctic ice cap like Leviathan, but we don't know how to live in the world we're in.

Supposing tonight I told you that President Johnson had asked me to inform you that next week a space-ship was going to a new planet and he relied on us to choose who should populate that planet. We had to pick twenty people. Now obviously all of us, if we went, would make that planet such a pattern for the earth that everybody would wish to go there. But leave us aside. Where would you choose those twenty from?

I'm what is called a Westerner. I come from a country that

calls itself Christian and a nation of faith. Out of the West in my lifetime have come two world wars, Fascism, Hitlerism and the social and economic injustices, too long tolerated, which gave Karl Marx his philosophy and provided the fuel and fire of Lenin, Stalin and now Khrushchev. And you see these colossal cracks appearing in the Communist façade. Where are you going to get people to populate a new world?

I was given a horrid warning when I came to Florida. I was told whatever you do, don't mention Cuba. Well, I am going to be bold and mention it. I want to tell you what I personally feel about Cuba and the colossal chance that situation offers to the American people in general and to the people of Florida in particular, if we dare to take it.

Now before Cuba fell there was no Russian military base on that island. There was an American military base. There were no Russian rubles in Cuba. There were a lot of American dollars. There were no Russians in the brothels and bars of that island, but some of us were there. Yet, with an idea touching human hearts, a Red hand stretched in and took that island.

What will suit Castro best? It is simply this. If the British continue to criticize the Americans for selling wheat to Russia and the Americans continue to criticize the British for selling buses to Cuba; if we have a continuation of interfraternal strife and violence between management and labor in the free world; if we talk about our liberties and have moral compromise and concubines in our homes; if we maintain a divided society which talks of individual liberty but robs individuals of liberty by our customs; if we keep on eternally blaming each other for the past and refusing to take up the challenge of the future—that is what will suit Mr. Castro best.

I believe it is our failure in the West to comprehend the

nature of this ideological struggle, and to pay the price of winning it, that has put that island into the Communist camp. I say this as a man who feels very, very deeply the sufferings of the Cubans. I do not believe we shall recapture Cuba for freedom without either a major war or an ideological thrust.

What do you think Russia wants that island for? Do you think it is just to point missiles at the heart of America? Or do you think it is as the launching pad for a tremendous ideological offensive right through Latin America and reaching up into the heart of your own country? The missiles may have been removed. The ideological offensive goes on relentlessly. Russia's prestige and power is at stake in Cuba.

I come from a country that for years was an imperial power. I happen to believe that, though we made many mistakes through our selfishness and our frailties, by and large we did our best. I believe that through education, environment and emancipation there are people in Africa and Asia today in charge of free countries who, unless we had given them our best, with all our faults, today might still be living in jungles and in huts. Now I do not believe in imperialism. I do not believe in colonialism. What I know, however, is that if you get an imperialist power committed to the holding of an island, nothing short of war will remove that power. Too much prestige is at stake.

At the same time, I believe that Cuba could be freed, and I will tell you how. Supposing you in Florida undertook the task which years ago we offered you, to be responsible for the moral re-armament of every Latin American land. You thought we were so foolish when we warned you—and we did. We warned you again and again and again and again and again that this thing was coming. You liked us, some of you. Some of you didn't. But you went on selfishly, comfortably, hoping to remain undisturbed. Ladies and gentlemen, if that goes on much longer, this thing is going to overwhelm the free world.

I just want to give you one example. I have been in Burma. That is a police state under General Ne Win, and the young Chinese Communists are the advisors of the Cabinet. They run the show. I saw them at work. In Burma in the hot weather the temperature is around 110. It is humid. Those young Chinese Communists were at work every morning at 7:30 as smart as whips, like American marines on parade. The men and women lived straight. They did not drink. They did not smoke. They were disciplined. That was not because they are better than we are. Nor because Communism is a better faith than the faith of free men. Communism is an evil faith. It was because they were willing to sacrifice more for their idea than we are willing to sacrifice for ours. Heaven help us!

The Communists know, in a Buddhist country, that if visitors go there talking big but living together in promiscuity, necking, flirting, bedding down at night, if they get drunk, if they puff away all the time, the Buddhists don't like it. Therefore the Communists live straight. Have we got men and women in the free world who love freedom enough to pay the price of discipline and change in our own lives to secure it, not just for our own country now, but for a continent?

Remember what happened when we did send a force out of Florida. We brought some Japanese, and you were generous hosts. I'll tell you what went into their training. We invited them to this country and we lived with them day and night for three months. There were 104 of them. When they arrived, all of them without exception were anti-American. Most of them were Marxist-trained. You could talk about the American way of life, you could sing the national anthem. They laughed at you. We had to deal with things like incest, adultery, abortion, bribery, theft, blackmail. All but two of them changed.

Do you realize what they have done? They went to Latin America. We financed them. We sold our life insurance policies. We sold our jewelry. Some of us sold our homes to send them there. The airlines—I like them, but they didn't help. Industrialists—I love them, but if you think there was big money coming from the mysterious industrialists, you're wrong. Not a dollar. The labor unions—I thank God for the standard of life the labor unions have achieved, but they didn't help.

Those Japanese went into Latin America. They tackled some of the toughest universities in countries like Peru, Chile and Brazil. They raised a force of Latin Americans who wrote a play called "El Condor." They took that play to Italy. I have just been in Rome. I have seen some of the leaders of the Church. They told me—now this is their opinion, not mine—that the work of those Latin Americans, changed by the Japanese you sent forth from Florida, has affected the life of millions of people in Italy. They say that it has taken root in the south and has begun to spread of its own accord. They beg us to go back with further forces, and at this moment we have a play and a force operating powerfully in Italy and winning colossal attention.

Then those Latin Americans brought their play to Canada —to French Canada, to Quebec. If you read the newspapers of Canada, they say that those Latin Americans ideologically are bringing an answer to the terrible divisions existing between the French and the English Canadians. It's a start. It isn't a finish. They are coming to Florida. Then they are go-

ing to Mexico. Then they are going south. What are you going to do with them? Supposing you had at last from Florida
men and women who said: "It takes an ideology to win an
ideological war. We cannot win without it. Our first step
ideologically is to give a passionate, deep, swift answer to
Communism right through Latin America. To give everyone
the hope of a greater revolution than this narrow, small class
concept which is bound in the end to lead to atomic war."

Supposing you raise a thousand people here, willing to pay
the price in their own lives of taking such a force down to
these countries in the south. You could do something that
would alter the history of the planet. And if you had that
colossal ideological blast coming from Latin America into
Cuba, that situation would change very swiftly. You criticize Castro. Fine. But you also have the Russians there, and
if you think they are going to be blown out of Cuba by pulling Castro's beard you are very much mistaken. You are
dealing with something much more powerful, much more
tough and much more world-wide.

At this moment fourteen African countries are asking
Moral Re-Armament to send forces to that continent.
Makarios the Greek, and Kutchuk the Turk, have begged me
to send a force to Cyprus. We can't do it because we haven't
got the money. We don't complain, but we give all we have
got. The royalties for the books and plays I have written since
the war have amounted to something like $1,250,000. I give
the copyright of the books and plays to Moral Re-Armament
before they are published, of course. I don't want to make a
cent out of it, and I don't take a cent of salary.

In America we mean to take 2,000 young Americans to
Mackinac Island this year. We will be there from June
through September. We mean to train those young Ameri-

cans ideologically with a purpose in life, a passion to pursue it, and the power of Almighty God to give them the discipline we all need so they can go out into Latin America, Africa, Asia or even the great cities of the United States and end division, answer corruption and give an idea superior to Communism. You cannot answer an idea with a bullet or a bomb or pounds or dollars or singing the national anthem or waving a flag or even a Cross. Those things have all been tried. The only answer to an idea is a superior idea lived with dedication by people who believe in it and will sacrifice for it. There is no other answer on earth.

America's new aim must be a new maturity that the hour demands. She can no longer live, think and dance a dream of politics in a 1936 pre-war outmoded style. A nation's thinking must rove and march ahead of history if she is to lead humanity on. America must, can and will under the direction of Almighty God lead us all forward along highways of freedom to secure the peace and build a new world. It will cost us many viewpoints as well as our selfishness and pride, but it will save civilization. Nations will leap and run to follow that new America, and our children and our children's children will rise up from end to end of the earth, Communist and non-Communist alike, and call this nation blessed because you have taught mankind how to live.

11

"Unless we deal with human nature thoroughly and drastically on a colossal scale, then nations which today gleam with wealth and glitter with the trappings of power may find they have been racing down the historic road to division, decadence and disaster."

Not by Wheat Alone

Chateau Laurier, Ottawa
January 20, 1964

A MAN IS BORN as he is. He may be black, white, brown, yellow, rich, poor, royal or rabble. For some reason this does not prevent certain people blaming others for the black of their skin, or the blue of their blood. This has always seemed to me foolish, yet I must admit that it is an attitude in which I myself sometimes share. I am proud that a trickle of Canada runs in my veins. It is a thin trickle, but firm. My great-grandparents sailed from Europe to Halifax, Nova Scotia. And for that reason, it is a particular privilege and honor to find myself speaking in Ottawa before so distinguished an audience tonight.

Avec votre permission, je veux ajouter que je me compte moitié français. Ma femme était française d'adoption. Nous nous sommes mariés en France à Marseilles. Je trouve qu'il y a un espoir vrai pour un Anglo-Saxon comme moi s'il est marié à une Latine. La moitié de moi, française, c'est ma meilleure moitié.

I also take pride in calling a great Canadian my friend. I mean the greatest Canadian of this century, Lord Beaverbrook. He trained and taught me in the Black Art, the art of the ink of newspapers. He has remained for more than thirty

131

years a man for whom I have not just admiration but affection.

He is the greatest Canadian of all, for three reasons. First, aircraft. When Britain was gasping for life and in deadly danger, Churchill clawed the enemy aircraft from the skies. He could never have done it unless Lord Beaverbrook had grown those claws. Britain would never have won the war without Churchill. Churchill would never have won the war without Beaverbrook's energy, ruthlessness and genius at getting machines out of factories and from people who declared they had already produced more than could possibly be produced.

Beaverbrook's second great claim to immortality is his vision of Empire, of Commonwealth. He saw that vast community of nations with many languages, many races, many backgrounds stretching to the far corners of the earth, all united with a common loyalty, not just to the Crown but to the ideals of service, faith and freedom that the best of Britain has always represented. He saw what that Commonwealth should have done, could have done, and, in my view, yet may do for the future of humanity. He hoped that my country, Britain, would be captured by the gleam of that vision, and follow the torch which day by day for years he himself upheld in the pages of the Express Newspapers.

Britain turned aside from that beckoning flame. Canada— uniquely equipped by history to speak to East and West alike —still has the chance of taking upon herself the leadership of a Commonwealth and Empire that could teach all nations how to live. The chance has almost but not quite vanished. I still hope Canada may see in the British Commonwealth and Empire her future hope of leadership and service to the world. For be sure of this. No nation, whether it be Canada or Britain, can in these troubled times float between East and West. Any nation which floats will surely sink. We need nations who will rise and decide to turn the tide of history before the tide of history sweeps us into the forgotten shifting sands of its bottomless oceans.

The third of Beaverbrook's achievements is the fight he at present wages for the character of my country, Britain. It was Browning who said: "I was ever a fighter, so one fight more, the best and the last." Whether this is Beaverbrook's last fight, I doubt. It is certainly his best. All ancient virtues, even the faith in Christianity which has been the strength of British home life, British integrity, British courage, are being assailed, questioned and undermined today. The assaults come from certain sections of the Press, certain television and broadcasting programs, even from the pulpits of certain beatnik bishops and perverted priests. Beaverbrook, through his Press, stands four-square for faith in God, and honor in man, at a time when these things are not necessarily as popular as once they were. He stands frontally against godlessness and dirt. Millions in Britain honor him for it.

I was interested in an editorial which appeared in one of his newspapers sustaining and supporting men who fought for the moral re-armament of Britain. It described the work in which my friends and I are engaged as seeking to establish consciousness of the Crucified Christ in the affairs of nations. That is one of the most pregnant and far-seeing descriptions of this work that I have read.

My country and the whole free world is in grave danger. I read somewhere that man cannot live by selling wheat alone. A house built on sand cannot last. A civilization built on dirt cannot endure. If men believe we can long last solely pursuing wealth, sex, comfort, dreading atomic desolation, in a climate which seeks to prove that evil is good, good evil —then men are mad. Those who concentrate upon the purse and belly of a national economy but neglect the ideas in the head, the answers in the heart, the soul and spirit of nations, do so at their peril. The prayer that has become common to the heart of humanity says: "Give us this day our daily bread." And: "Thy kingdom come, Thy will be done." The first phrase is a need. The second, a purpose.

In Britain our danger is not the loss of Empire but the loss of purpose, the loss of aim, the loss of something great to live for which all men know and all men can love.

Twenty years after the French Revolution men succeeded in enthroning a harlot on the High Altar of Notre Dame. Today we worship stars of the screen for no other reason than their various and much-publicized acts of infidelity. Stars like this are a poor alternative to the Star of Bethlehem which for centuries at least we professed to pursue and follow.

We have in Edinburgh a cheap crew who pushed a naked lady in a wheelbarrow in front of a public audience and called it culture. It is lavatory art. Thank heaven the public stomach has heaved against this type of filth and spewed it forth from its mouth. I understand you have dirty birds here who say they don't mind their daughters sleeping with people, provided they sleep in beds and not in automobiles. I hope Canada will not make heroes out of men like that as we do out of some of our muck-mongers. I hope you will not tolerate leadership in your churches by those who want to cut Christ down to suit the compromise and comfort of modern man, instead of holding modern man up to the everlasting challenge and cure of Christ on the Cross. Christ not only forgives but cures. So many people nowadays want to exploit His forgiveness by pretending His cure no longer works.

Unless men at the head of our affairs seek the ways of God again and let it be known that those ways are sought, unless we deal with human nature thoroughly and drastically on a colossal scale, then nations which today gleam with wealth and glitter with the trappings of power and influence may find they have been reeling, racing and sliding down the historic road to division, decadence and disaster.

Now much is happening to offset this trend of our time. I remain full of hope. I want to tell you some of the news, and good news, that is being made around the world.

We have just come from India. There Rajmohan Gandhi, grandson of Mahatma Gandhi, has been leading a nation-wide action to rouse the conscience of his people and to create a moral revolution that will offset the danger that he sees of disintegration and dictatorship in his land. I want to read to you from a letter which I received a few days ago outlining the situation in India:

"The Minister of Food and Agriculture, who is re-garded as a middle-of-the-road man, told the leading columnist of the country he wanted immediate national-ization of the banks and of import and export. Krishna Menon and Malaviya, two men sympathetic to Com-munism, are leading a relentless, expanding battle for these objectives, and although the majority of Congress Parliamentarians and Congress leaders in the provinces are opposed to these objectives, it looks as if they will surrender.

"Their next target is the Press. The new line is that the proprietors must not have any say in the policy of the newspapers and that editors should be forced to curtail their views. Intellectuals and professors nominated by the Government should control the policy and thinking of the newspapers.

"I am weighing carefully what I should do. If Congress leaders do not now assert themselves and arrest this bank nationalization move, we shall be steamrollered into the situation that now prevails in Ceylon and Burma. It may well be that I should soon launch a vigorous campaign against the move."

Moral Re-Armament is a plumb line drawn by God through the heart of modern man. It is the test by which God judges individuals and society. Men and nations will rise or fall, grow in character, or shrink in personality according as they accept that challenge or reject it. I have faith in the common man. I believe that when the crisis of our times grows more acute and more clear, he will accept the challenge, he will be willing to pay the price of change, he will understand that there is nobody more reactionary, whether Communist or non-Communist, than the person who wants to see the world different but refuses to become different himself.

Lenin once said: "My observations during my years of exile in Switzerland led me to consider the cultivated strata in the capitalist countries of Western Europe and America as deaf mutes. We must act accordingly." He has acted accordingly. He and Stalin believed that the West would dig their own grave in Asia and Africa. I do not believe that we are nations of deaf mutes in the West. I think we can open our ears and eyes to what is happening around us. I believe we have a voice clear enough to speak in such a way that the whole earth will listen and follow. At the same time, it is not always made easy. Mark Twain once said that a lie would travel round the world while truth was putting on its pants. And it is true that in the work in which I am engaged some knaves pass out lies for fools to swallow, and the fools swallow them.

In Canada I have met people of great charm who do much harm. I have met men of integrity and intelligence, but with an ignorance that strikes me as vast and perilous. They seem to swallow smear as geese eat grass—and leave a trail behind them.

We are accused of exaggeration. For example, it is said that we played no part in ending the EOKA killings in Cyprus. Dame Flora MacLeod and the rest of us passed through Cyprus in October. President Makarios, the Greek, Vice-President Kutchuk, the Turk, both gave receptions for us. Both consulted privately with me and both urged me to bring a force of Moral Re-Armament speedily to the island in her present difficulties, because of the part we played in settling the earlier trouble.

On the day Cyprus became free, Makarios and Kutchuk sent the first flag of the new nation ever to leave the country to Dr. Buchman at Caux as their tribute to what had been achieved.

Incidentally, the gentleman from my country who invented this story of an exaggeration over Cyprus is the same man who, in EOKA days, was telling the Cypriots: "You'll only get the British out with bullets. That's the only language they understand."

Some people say we are pacifist. In the sense that we love peace this is true. In the sense that we believe in unilateral disarmament or that we would refuse to fight in war for the things we hold most dear, it is a lie and always has been a lie. My only brother fought all through the last war and, I am proud to say, fought at the side of the Canadians. He finally laid down his life at Arnhem with the paratroops. In Britain, my friends in Moral Re-Armament won every decoration for valor that can be awarded, including the Victoria Cross.

Some people say we are secretive about money. It is a lie. The truth is that in Somerset House, England, the accounts of Moral Re-Armament have been filed for the last twenty-five years. They are audited each year by Price, Waterhouse & Co. Anybody, for the sum of one shilling, can inspect them.

It is alleged that labor is against us because the International Confederation of Free Trade Unions passed a resolution against us. It is a lie. The truth is that three members of the executive in 1953 at Stockholm prepared a resolution. The executive took no action about it. It was not even put to the Congress. Nevertheless, a lie was leaked to the Press by our enemies on the executive which the world has often believed and which suggests that the I.C.F.T.U. passed some resolution against us at that conference.

But the story I want to deal with this evening is the story concerning Adolf Hitler. Some people believe Dr. Buchman was a supporter of Hitlerism. It is a lie. One sentence quoted out of context which he is alleged to have uttered in the year 1936 is used against us all. He is said to have said: "I thank God for a man like Adolf Hitler who has raised a frontline of defense against the anti-Christ of Communism." I was not there in 1936. I have no idea whether Dr. Buchman spoke as reported or not. He never met Hitler. And certainly I find it strange that on a day when he was interviewed by over fifty reporters, only one of them reported him in this sense.

I knew Frank Buchman well. I worked with him closely for fifteen years. His whole life was dedicated to answering the materialism, the moral compromise and corruption out of which rose the filthy apparatus of the Gestapo, the hideous treatment of the Jews, the foul satanic regime that all decent men hated and that millions of decent men hazarded their lives to destroy. Taking one slanted sentence out of a press interview in 1936 and using it to try and indict a work of God throughout the modern world seems to me a poor way to judge the life work of a man who won countless thousands to a faith in God and to an experience of Christ.

Hitler's Gestapo issued instructions to the Nazi military authorities to smash Moral Re-Armament wherever they found it. I have in my safe the printed book of Gestapo instructions—122 pages of them. There the Gestapo say that Moral Re-Armament "frontally opposed the Swastika with the Cross of Christ." It had become their "avowed antagonist," and was lending "the Christian garment to world democratic aims."

But I would like now to read you one or two things that other people said about Hitler. Here is somebody speaking in 1935:

"Hitler may go down in history as the man who restored honor to the great Germanic nation and led it back serene, hopeful and strong to the forefront of the European family circle."

Who do you think this was? None other than Winston Churchill. Does anybody dare to suggest he was a Nazi?

Then here is another statement: "Hitler is the George Washington of his country." That was Lloyd George. Bless his heart, Lloyd George was many things. But nobody who knew that wise, wily wizard would dare to suggest he was Fascist or Nazi.

In the mid-thirties the Catholic Bishops of Germany issued a pastoral letter which was read in all the churches: "Catholics will not find it difficult to appreciate the new powerful movement of authority in the new German state and to subordinate themselves to it." Does anyone dare to suggest that the Roman Catholic Church sponsored a regime which spilt the blood of Catholic martyrs in many a city and many a land?

In August 1934, the association of national German Jews issued an appeal in support of Hitler. It stated: "Despite the fact that it brought hardships in its train, we welcomed the national rising in January 1933, because we regarded it as the only way to repair the damage caused in fourteen years of misfortune by un-German elements." I hope nobody is going to suggest that the Jewish people whose sufferings still scream aloud in the terrors of this dark century, whose blood and bravery still challenge the conscience of every decent man in the world, were Hitler lovers. Of course not. Every sane man knew the reason the German Jews issued that statement was because they were trying to avoid the hell of the gas chambers, the devilish devices of the cellars of the Gestapo. Who can blame them?

But remember that Buchman, too, had people in Germany who trusted him and who felt that in Moral Re-Armament lay the answer to Hitlerism and to Stalinism. How could Buchman, when needled and pressured by this distorted statement torn from its context, come out and say, as of course he believed: "Hitler is a madman to behave in this foul, sadistic and irreparable way. All the trappings of Nazidom must be torn aside and thrown onto the rubbish heap of history. We must never again tolerate this infamy in the midst of man." Had he said it, everybody in Germany known to have had any contact with him would instantly have been destroyed. And indeed many of them were destroyed.

I tell you these things so you may understand the folly of believing the kind of smears that come our way as we fight to challenge the motives of every man and every nation and to redirect history.

Some nation has got to rise and answer the challenge of history. Some nation has got to say to the listening earth: "In our society we have answered the divisions that will destroy humanity. We have learned to live like sons and daughters of God because we are guided by the Living God. Our homes are united, our families are united, our women are pure, our industries are honorable, labor and management both serve the community, both put people before profits, wages or hours. We have decided in an age that has turned its back on God to live as God wanted men to live. We reject the concept that man created God and now can abolish Him. We accept humbly, hopefully, the truth that God made man and now can change him and lead nations and continents in the paths of peace."

Canada might be that nation.

12

*"One state legislature free from fear
of men, committed not just to do
the right as God grants us to see the
right, but to legislate and agitate
so that what is right becomes the
norm of modern America, will give
to nations the secret of freedom
that endures, and to the world point
the highroad to lasting peace."*

Design for Dedication

The Senate of the
Commonwealth of Massachusetts
March 4, 1964

Introduction by the Honorable John E. Powers,
President of the Massachusetts Senate:

LIEUTENANT GOVERNOR BELLOTTI and members, constitutional officers, very distinguished group of my fellow citizens: First of all I am extremely happy that you are here in this very historic body, the Massachusetts Senate, because, after being in government for a period of a quarter of a century and soon to depart from these nostalgic chambers, I believe that the presence of our invited guest here today is of tremendous significance to all of us.

Each day preceding our sessions Monsignor Christopher Griffin, our chaplain, leads us in a most meaningful prayer to ask Divine Guidance that whatever our deliberations will be, affecting as they do the five and a half million of our fellow citizens, they be the result of an honest interchange of ideas and ideals. So it is rather coincidental that on this occasion, when I look back over twenty-five years, I have the privilege of having as a guest one of the most, in my opinion, outstanding, dedicated men of the world today. It is a dedication that is possessed of a tremendous amount of contagion.

A short time ago we had here in the Massachusetts Senate and House and in our Commonwealth both Johnny Sayre and Rusty Wailes, the two young Olympic stars who are traveling throughout the world trying to re-arm morally the whole world on the basis of the morals embodied in the play, "Space Is So Startling"— a play written by our guest of today.

I am encouraged because I had the privilege of presenting these two young men to the late President of the United States, and to have had him on the 19th day of October here in the City of Boston publicly thank them for their contribution to world understanding and for becoming the medium through which people would break down the barriers of misdirection and ignorance.

Peter Howard is one of the most remarkable men of this or any other era. Most mortals would be very proud and happy to attain distinction in one particular line of endeavor. Mr. Howard is one of those very rare individuals gifted by the Almighty with the talent to reach the top in everything to which they turn their hand. He is a champion sportsman, having captained both his Oxford University rugby football team and the English international team. He was also a member of the British bobsled quartet which broke the world's record some twenty-five years ago.

He became a political columnist for Lord Beaverbrook's papers in England and for a number of years was the conscience of his many readers. He is a distinguished author whose books have been printed in sixteen different languages. One of them, *Guilty Men,* played a significant part in mobilizing British opinion against appeasement and preparing the way for a Winston Churchill. He is a noted playwright, having written ten plays and collaborated in several others. Three of them have run for over two years in London; others have been performed all over the world. His latest, "Space Is So Startling," which some of you saw in conjunction with our national state legislative leaders' conference last fall, is now touring India. He is a forceful and articulate speaker, a fact which will be proved to you very shortly.

Peter Howard is in charge of the world program of Moral Re-Armament. In that capacity he has entrée into the homes, into the offices of the world's leaders. He is not a cleryman; he is not a politician. Yet I know that his remarks will appeal to all who have faith in God and to all of us who believe in and have worked for honest, decent and efficient government.

I am privileged, I am proud, I am honored in the presence of the Lieutenant Governor of this Commonwealth and you, distinguished members of the Senate, and you, my fellow citizens of the Commonwealth of Massachusetts, and visitors from beyond, to present to you Peter Howard.

IT IS A HIGH HONOR to be invited to address this historic body. To me, this place is hallowed ground. I feel as I do when my feet stand on the marble pavements of the Acropolis in Athens or tread the dust of the ancient Senate House of Rome. The fruit of freedom that millions yet enjoy sprang from roots in this Legislature, as from the council chambers and debating halls of Greece and Rome.

My delight at being in your midst today is due to the generous friendship and gracious invitation of Senator John Powers. As a man and Senator, his fame is known far beyond the borders of this state and indeed beyond the borders of the United States. He also is one of the most knowledgeable

men in the world on the subject of constitutional and par-
liamentary law. He informs me that your Massachusetts Constitution is one of the oldest of its type in the world and that
on it was based the American Constitution. And so the
branches of your tree have indeed spread from coast to coast
and across oceans.

We live in an age for heroes. No time has ever offered
man such perils or such prizes. Man can either provide a full
life for humanity, or destroy himself with the problems he
has created. The test of this century will prove to be whether
man matches the growth of wealth and power with the growth
of spirit and character—or whether, like an infant heedlessly
playing with terrible toys, he destroys the house he would
have inherited.

It was John Winthrop who, on the flagship *Arabella* three
hundred and thirty-four years ago, said to his shipmates:
"We shall be as a city upon a hill—the eyes of all people are
upon us." I am told and believe that what Massachusetts is
and does today, America will be and do tomorrow. It remains
true that the eyes of the earth are on this State. For where
America goes, the world goes. If America fails, the world
fails. If America succeeds in creating the new type of man
and the new type of society that the pace and pressure of the
hour demands, she will lead humanity onward in the next
stage of human evolution.

The late President Kennedy understood this. I make no
apology for mentioning his name in this his birthplace. For,
although I am a foreigner, your late son belonged to us all.
I met and talked with him in Washington about the work of
Moral Re-Armament. He understood it. It is true that, like
all men engaged in politics, he had his critics and his enemies.
It is true that in life he was more controversial than after his

insane assassination. Yet he comprehended the heart of the matter. He knew that men must be ready to sacrifice, sweat, strive and stride forward together into a new age of justice, brotherhood and sanity if civilization was not to perish.

His body rests at Arlington. His challenge still confronts every citizen of my country and of yours. It stands here in our midst valiant as the man himself, as real, difficult, fascinating as the Cross of his Master. It would be a mockery of his ideal if after his death we continued merely to praise, mourn or even glorify him, but went on living as many of us lived before—selfishly, comfortably, undisturbed.

We cannot all have the capacity of a John Kennedy. We can all be part of the design for dedication that he gave. It is to build a new America and a new world, and to accept the discipline that task demands. It is time now for us who have sorrowed at his tomb to bestir ourselves to follow the furrow that he drew across the earth and beyond the far horizon. It yet leads to a concept of society as different from the past as a modern Massachusetts hotel is from the plumbing of the *Arabella,* as definite in aim as were the men who first built here a new government on frontiers that then were perilous, and who later opened up a nation to the South and West.

Some have begun to do it. I have been marching in India with Rajmohan Gandhi, grandson of the Mahatma. He is twenty-eight years old. The enemy are within his country's gates to the North. To the South the state of Kerala, and the island of Ceylon beyond, are in danger. Gandhi says that his grandfather freed India from imperialism and helped Britain to remain India's friend. We left India. But our departure did not, alas, mean the end of all problems as many Indians had hoped.

Today, other countries in Asia, in Africa, are finding out

that most problems have two legs and that the color of those legs, black, yellow, brown or white, does not change the nature of the problem. Last year 63% of India's taxes were unpaid. The head of the railways says over $6,000,000 of cheated fares were discovered. Corruption and bribery have become nationwide. Divisions of caste and hate of race abound.

Gandhi led a 4,000-mile march through India. The response of the masses has been such as would delight any politician, Democrat or Republican, in election year. He has asked for 10,000 Indian youths to come to camps in the hills this spring and be trained in Moral Re-Armament.

A few days ago, speaking to 75,000 people on Chowpatty Sands, a traditional meeting place of his grandfather on the shores of the Arabian Ocean at Bombay, Gandhi said:

"We are determined to raise a force of able, intelligent young men and women who will live straight, who will not be corrupted by money or power, who can lead this nation. This can be done sooner than people think. Every weak link in the chain inside India must now be strengthened. Corruption, jealousy and division inside India are an open invitation to aggression.

"I am fed up by people who always accuse the Communists whenever anything goes wrong. There is a strike and we blame them. There is a fall in production and we blame them. Our children rebel and we blame them. Even if all the Communists of India became saints and went to the Himalayas, we would still have our problems with us.

"I am equally fed up by the idea that some have that every capitalist should be killed or thrown into this ocean. Many capitalists have been selfish. If they continue in their selfishness they will face violence. But our problems of poverty and inequality will still remain with us even if every rich man in Bombay or India is jailed or liquidated.

"Neither jailing Communists nor jailing capitalists will produce more wealth. Only work produces wealth. If capitalists continue to want more and more profit and work less and less, and eat and drink more and more, there won't be more wealth. If workers also imitate the capitalists and want more and more for less and less work, they help in raising prices of commodities which other workers and peasants have to buy.

"We must strengthen and increase the size of our armed forces. But we have to raise another kind of army too—an army of dedicated revolutionaries, men and women who attack injustice and corruption fearlessly because they are not afraid of the spotlight being thrown on them; men and women who do not shield other people's corruption; men and women who do not minimize the problems; men and women who will stand up firmly in front of the problem instead of running away from it; men and women who will apply rigorous standards of honesty, purity and unselfishness to their daily living; yes, and men and women who will boldly seek out the true voice of their heart, the Voice of God, and obey it.

"I do not invite you to walk on a comfortable road. I do not promise you all the luxuries of life. I promise you a fight far harder than anything the nation had to suffer in the freedom struggle. I will not insult you by assuming that you do not want to sacrifice. With sacrifice and fearlessness you and I will have to give this nation a new leadership."

Gandhi has been threatened with violence by the Communists of India. Why do they fear him? Because he knows something that the State Departments of the West have yet to comprehend. It is that you cannot kill an idea with a bullet, a bomb, a slogan, a national anthem, a flag or a Cross. For centuries men have tried and failed. Nor can you buy it off with pounds or dollars. In other words, free men cannot hope to win an ideological war without an ideology.

Gandhi is out not merely to contain or control the Communist world, but to change it. He believes that the philosophy of that old prayer, "Thy will be done on earth as it is in Heaven," if it becomes a commitment of muscle, mind and money, the motive of nations rather than a mere pious drone of sincere but ineffective individuals, is more revolutionary than anything concocted by Karl Marx.

Gandhi believes that on earth God's will is worked by men —men who listen to the Almighty and obey Him. He believes that political remedies, economic remedies, social remedies, remedies of education and environment all are necessary. All are urgent. But it takes more than laws to answer hate, cure fear, cancel greed and end the selfishness of race, class, color, background that divides us. Rules, laws, social and economic programs do not touch the intangibles of the heart.

Massachusetts with the threads of Yankee and immigrant, blueblood and egghead, fisherman and farmer, Irish and Italian and Jew, which your genius has woven into common texture, is able to speak to the earth. Heart power is the strength of America. Hate power is the weakness of this world.

Think of the Irish. I have an eighth of the Irish in me, which means that I am at least 12½% proud of my forebears. The Irish were treated like cattle. They were starved, shot, shunned, hounded and betrayed. Yet they have carried a leaven of love and humor wherever they go. I sometimes think Moral Re-Armament has much in common with the Irish—often misunderstood, always irresistible.

Lord Beaverbrook, one of the greatest hearts and truest friends Britain, America and the free world ever had, tells the tale that when the Irish troubles began, his friend, Bonar Law, had to answer questions about them in the House of Commons. With difficulty Beaverbrook reached Tim Healey by telephone in Dublin. Tim Healey was a friend of Bonar Law and Beaverbrook, but on the other side of the barricades. "Tim," said Beaverbrook, "Bonar has to answer questions in Parliament this afternoon. Tell me when did these troubles begin?" Healey replied: "When Strongbow came to Ireland." Beaverbrook laughed. He said: "That's all very well, but when are they going to end?" Replied Healey: "When Cromwell gets out of hell."

But there is an answer to problems that so long have bedeviled us. To nations like yours, and perhaps my own, is entrusted the moral leadership of the world. But we cannot offer moral leadership to nations if we have moral laxity in our homes, moral anarchy in industry, moral compromise in the private lives of public men.

There is no compulsion for anyone to enter public life. Every road in free society is open to every individual according to his capacity and choice. But if a man or woman decides to run for public office, then their private lives become the concern of the public. General David Shoup, as Commandant of the Marine Corps, addressing his men at Okinawa, put one side of this matter clearly when he said: "A man who can break or rationalize breaking the oath he gave before God and man when he repeated his marriage vows is a man who could, if he so desired, or was subject to severe pressure, rationalize breaking the oath he took when he became a commissioned officer in the U.S. Marine Corps. A man who can betray his wife and children for lustful purposes is a man who could betray his country for his own ends."

Where on earth are we going to create men fit to live in the modern world, or to build a new world? Man has grown up technologically and industrially. We have become industrial and technological giants able to smash continents, explore the stars, communicate with each other from continent to continent in words and ways undreamed of fifty years ago. But we have remained moral and spiritual pigmies. We endure a pill-and-thrill civilization, titivating our boredom with movies of sex and violence, dependent on pills for pep, pills for sleep, pills to relieve ulcers; often unable to unite a home, an industry or our own nation, let alone an earth torn asunder with fear, greed and hate.

It may fall to the lot of modern Massachusetts to fulfill the dream of the adventurers and pioneers who founded the Bay Colony. We have had whole nations captured by the iron control of Fascism and the steely cruelty of Communism. Not one state can yet say with honesty: "We are by choice as God-controlled in every section of our life as those dictatorships were and are, by compulsion, man-controlled."

It is not for me to question Supreme Court decisions. But no Supreme Court can prevent any heart, any home, any school, any industry, any assembly from obeying the guidance that a Supreme Being gives to conscience and to heart. The word of God may be kept by law out of schools. Then the words of the professors of anti-God should also, in my view, legally be silenced; those teachers and professors who use their so-called intellectuality to confuse and destroy the faith of youth. I am sure of this; whatever happens or does not happen in schools and colleges, if we curb God in the upbringing of our children, as we curb dogs in our streets, we are on the road to tyranny.

A great American President used to tell the story of a room with two doors. One door was small and narrow and led to an uphill stairway. It was always closed. Nobody used it. People were told that it had had its day, it had become dangerous. Man had learned too much to need it any more. The other door was wide and tall and easy. It was a swing door which went wherever it was pushed. It led to a downhill corridor. One day there was fire in the building. There was an earthquake. The whole place shook and was in danger. People panicked and cried aloud. They rushed to the wide, easy door. It was jammed and immovable. In a crisis it had failed. Then somebody as a last hope tried the other door. It had been unlocked all the time. It led them instantly to safety.

The wide door is called the "Philosophy of Materialism." Through it, all down history, have been carried the biers of dead liberties and the blood-stained banners of tyranny triumphant. The narrow door may be called the "Tradition of Massachusetts." Puritan and Pilgrim built that heritage. William Penn described it when he said: "Men must choose to be governed by God, or they condemn themselves to be ruled by tyrants."

Why not a state governed by men governed by God? Modern society is so in love with what other people think that it yields its conviction about what is right. We need to heed again the challenge of that tinker, that Puritan, that "square" of yesterday who from Bedford Gaol in my country sent forth a challenge that rings down the ages. John Bunyan wrote:

> "Who would true valor see
> Let him come hither;
> One here will constant be,
> Come wind, come weather;
> Then fancies fly away;
> He'll fear not what men say;
> He'll labor night and day
> To be a pilgrim."

One state legislature free from fear of what men say, committed not just to do the right as God grants us to see the right, but to legislate and agitate so that what is right becomes the norm of modern America, will give once more to nations the secret of freedom that endures, and to the world point the highroad to lasting peace.

Asked—and Answered

A lively question-and-answer period followed most of Peter Howard's addresses. Some of the more frequently repeated questions are included here. They are arranged by subject matter—foreign policy, politics and national life, economics, morals and religion, and ideology. Some are broad in scope, others deal with topics of the moment. All served to stimulate replies which developed Mr. Howard's central themes.

Foreign Policy

Question: How have free men let themselves be used to establish Castros around the world?

Answer: Here is a personal illustration. My colleagues and I went to some of the biggest New York investors in Cuba one year before Castro took command. I dared to tell them that Castro was a committed Communist. He was going to take over the country and run America out of Cuba. They treated me with the contempt that any foreigner rightly deserves who ventures to stick his nose into somebody else's business. They said: "You don't understand anything about Castro. We understand him very well. We know perfectly well the reforms he stands for are the right reforms and we're going to stick with him."

Then they asked: "If you wanted to give an ideological answer to Castro on Cuba, how much would it cost?" I answered: "To give the right idea and the moral basis to secure freedom on Cuba would cost a million dollars." They showed me politely out. They gave Castro eight million dollars. Your government gave him fourteen million dollars and he skinned the whole blooming lot.

Q: Does the win-and-lose record of American diplomacy in the past twenty years warrant De Gaulle or anyone else entrusting their interests to the United States?

A: America, without seeking it, has had world leadership dumped on her lap. America has risen to that responsibility in a phenomenal way. I marvel at how this mighty country, up till now so self-sufficient and safe, has suddenly taken on with the cognizance of all her people an intelligent, progressive, world responsibility. But America needs help in her world plans. If America said to Africa, to Asia and even to Europe, "We are going to build the right kind of world. We need your help to do it," the black men, the yellow men, the brown men, the red men, even the white men like myself would rise up and say: "We will come with you on that basis to the ends of the earth."

Q: What country is best equipped to dip into political affairs outside their own borders, direct others as to how to govern and install the best system of government?

A: The whole future of the world depends on the United States. All of us know, if we are sensible and honest, that we owe our present freedom to your country. All of us know that any hopes we have of freedom in the future depend on you. I don't think "meddling" in political affairs in other countries is right. What is needed is a revolutionary concept for the whole earth. That is the missing element in statesmanship. When you have that, you will get freedom marching across the earth again.

Q: Would recognition of Red China tend to ease or to intensify tensions in Asia?

A: My country was one of the first to recognize Red China. I think Chiang Kai-shek is one of the most abused and misused men of modern history. Certain elements of the world press have assassinated the character of men like Chiang, Diem, or anybody else who stands in their path, often for ideological reasons. I think if Red China is recognized, you will have a potent Chinese minority in every Asian country who will turn to Peking and no more look to Washington. But the pressures are building up. If we had had an ideology ten years ago, we would very soon have had a situation where nation after nation would have been revolutionized in the right way and you would now have Communism on the retreat everywhere. And I still think there is time to do it.

Q: Is America right in trying to keep Red China out of the U.N.?

A: I think that I would be unwise to try and dictate policy to the United States of America. General de Gaulle is very keen to try to get Red China into the United Nations and to keep Britain out of the Common Market. Many English people would like him to reverse his ploys.

I would like to see any free man, or any free nation, with an ideology so powerful that you could enlist, challenge and change any Communist you confronted. I'm absolutely fed up with this idea that we've got to console the Communist world or contain the Communist world or keep the Communist world out. I want to see us change and enlist the Communist world in the next step forward in human evolution. I believe many Communists are hungry to do it. But it will need a mighty change in us first.

Q: Was Madame Nhu right in what she told U.S. audiences, and what do you think will happen to Madame Nhu if she is extradited to South Vietnam?

A: If Madame Nhu is extradited to South Vietnam, unless she goes under the protection of America, she will be killed.

A lot of us have difficult female relatives, and it is a characteristic that they often open their mouths and talk too loudly through them. But, basically, I think Madame Nhu was right. What that woman stood for in Vietnam was the best hope America had of winning that war. If you are going to slaughter every politician because he has two or three difficult relatives, there will be a mighty slaughter around town, and not only in Vietnam.

Q: Did the press give an accurate picture of Diem, and if not, why?

A: The answer is no. The correspondents were in a city a long way from home, where French is spoken, where it's tremendously hot, where there are very few comforts. It's not a shack city, but it's not like New York. The brothels were closed because it was wartime, and you couldn't get a drink. Some of the foreign correspondents got extremely frustrated and they hated what they called the puritanical nature of the regime. So they turned on Diem. Diem, a month or six weeks before he was killed, actually made considerable concessions to the demands being made upon him by the military authorities. That was never printed in the Western press.

I don't mean those men were sinister agents. But it suited the Communists to get rid of Diem. And some newspapermen there didn't understand ideology. What they did understand was the creature demands of pressmen who work hard and want whisky and women. There were very clever men who worked on their desires and frustrations and got them to project their hostility on to Diem. You didn't get the true story then, and you've not had it since.

Q: Do you agree with the United Nations?

A: I agree with the idea of the U.N. I think it's fine, but without a change in human nature the ideals of the U.N. will never be achieved. It is called the United Nations, but if you've been there you will know it is deeply divided. You find organized blocs of disagreement, and not just between the Communist and anti-Communist camps. Until that is changed, it is juvenile to expect the U.N. to unite the world.

Q: Is there anything the United States could have done,

considering how powerful, how wealthy we are, that would have made us loved by everybody?

A: It is of course true that some countries are jealous of America. It's no good pretending in my country, if we see ourselves encouraged rapidly out of Asia, out of Africa, out of the places where we once held sway, that we're not somewhat pleased if we see the Americans making mistakes. It's not very pleasant, but it's very human.

But I don't think the point is whether America is loved or not loved. I believe that if the whole world rose up today and said, "Good old America," it wouldn't alter the price of cheese. I don't think America knows what the world expects, and rightly expects, of her. The whole world is waiting for America to show humanity how to take the next step forward in human evolution.

Q: What do you think about the Peace Corps?

A: Would you like me to be polite, or honest? I think the Peace Corps is a splendid idea, and it represents the best idealism of the United States. I salute it. But, and it is a big but, I am not sure that the Peace Corps is given adequate training when it is sent forth.

If you are going to send out a Peace Corps in the modern world, you've got to teach them to live straight, otherwise they are inadequately equipped to deal with the real problems of the country.

In one important Asian country the man who leads the Peace Corps is to my knowledge a hard-core, highly intelligent Communist. Things like this give other nations a slightly distorted picture. I wish the whole Peace Corps was morally re-armed.

What these underprivileged countries need are revolutionary Americans who go in there and say: "We understand Marx and Communism. We understand you. We've got a far bigger plan for you and your country, and we've got the discipline to see you achieve it." If you can send out a Peace Corps like that, you can win the world.

Q: You said: "I thank God for the armed strength of the United States." Do you also thank God for the armed strength of the Soviet Union?

A: I thank God there is a power balance which means no selfish nation risks trying to overcome the world with its armed strength. I would thank God far more forcibly if men learned to live without arms. I think people who talk about atomic war as a solution to modern problems are insane.

Q: How do you reconcile unselfishness and love with piling up atomic weapons?

A: I do not believe we would help the cause of freedom or faith by leaving the free world disarmed. I want America to stay strong. Freedom in the world depends upon it. But I think in addition America needs an idea in her head, which is sadly lacking in my country, and an answer in her heart, which is also sadly lacking in most countries—an answer to selfishness and hate and dirt.

Q: What do you think of pacifism?

A: I'm no pacifist, because I believe there are things worse than death and I would rather die than see those things happening to you and me, and to your nation and mine. Of course I want peace in the world. But what is the intelligent way to obtain it? Adenauer, when he was Chancellor, said at a press conference: "Unless the work of Moral Re-Armament is extended, peace in the world cannot be preserved." Peace is not just an idea. It is people becoming different.

Q: Is there always a right and a wrong in an international dealing?

A: I know there always is in a personal dealing, and I strongly suspect there is in an international dealing. I believe that some nation has got to stand four square in the modern world and say: "Right is right, wrong is wrong, and we stand for the right, as God gives us to see the right, in our international policies, in our private lives and in our national policies." If you go to international conferences, the problems sitting around the table are far more pressing than the problems sitting on the table. People spend hours, weeks and months discussing the problems on the table, but the problems around the table remain completely unchanged. Human nature doesn't shift, because nobody tackles it.

Politics and National Life

Q: What would you predict of the European reaction if Barry Goldwater were elected President in 1964?

A: I believe that all free countries should elect their own Prime Ministers and Presidents without interference from overseas. I have fullest confidence in the wisdom of choice of the United States of America. Don't you tell us who should be our Prime Minister and we won't tell you who should be your President!

Q: Are you suggesting that the State Department is Communist-infiltrated?

A: If you ask me whether I think you have highly trained Communists in the State Department, my answer is simply, yes. I'm bound to say I think our British Foreign Office showed you the way to do it. I love my country deeply. I want to make this very plain, because people have such an odd idea nowadays of patriotism. I believe that you should love your country as it is, deeply, but fight to help your country become the country it's meant to be. In my country we've had Burgess, MacLean, Philby—we've had story after story of men who through moral laxity have been captured and won to Communism, and there at the heart of our nation have given secrets to people who are our enemies. I do not believe that you can tackle this problem without a mighty moral revolution. That's what we need and, to be quite honest, I know you need it in the State Department.

Q: What can each one of us do to bring the ideology of Moral Re-Armament to those who govern our countries?

A: This year people are looking for votes, I'm told. And I think it would be very good if in every community there was a strong force of people who said very frankly to the men in public life: "We want the best basis of freedom in America. We want a morally rearmed America. We want to know where you stand on that point." The second thing, I think, is to see that some of the best of your youth come to Mackinac for training. We want the best. We want them there for two and a half months.

The third point is very simply this—that a nation gets the government it deserves. And you cannot expect people who live as they please to elect public men whose private lives are impeccable. We need an incorruptible Washington, and a nation demanding moral re-armament from every person who seeks a vote.

Q: Does Moral Re-Armament proceed from the personal to the political?

A: The whole world needs an aim greater than anything Communism or anti-Communism produces. Nationalism is too small an aim. If you want the world to get straight, you cannot be effective in that revolution unless you are at least willing to get straight yourself. But you do not have to wait till you are straight before you can participate in a revolution.

Politics, yes, if you mean by politics the way in which legislation, government, cabinet, affect the lives of people. But we would never be a political party, nor would we ever be exlusively for one party. We believe that every party needs this spirit—every single one.

Q: Is your strategy to touch as many of the leaders of the influential countries as possible?

A: We have a world work that is active in most countries and growing. Naturally, if we get to men who are able by their actions and their motives to affect the lives of thousands of other people, we try and give them the biggest aim and the most revolutionary motive we can. But to suggest, as some people do, that we concentrate on big names and important people is rubbish. It so happens, at an Assembly such as we have in Odawara, for example, in Japan, or Caux in Switzerland, or Mackinac in the United States, if 10,000 people and four Prime Ministers come, the press mentions the Prime Ministers.

But our job is concerned with everybody. And most of them are ordinary people—in their hundreds of thousands.

Q: How can absolute moral standards be applied in politics, which is in part the art of compromise?

A: A man in politics must achieve the very best he can with the society in which he is working, and therefore he often has to compound with something less than the maximum. But if every man in Parliament refused to compromise with standards of absolute honesty, purity, unselfishness and love, in any situation, we would get far better laws.

Economics

Q: Does Moral Re-Armament have an economic program?

A: Yes, our economic program is very simple: It is madness to live in a world quite capable of filling every stomach with food, of giving everybody a decent place to live, of giving everybody the education and background they must have—unless we tackle these needs swiftly, radically, immediately.

Q: Can you legislate these things in a democratic system?

A: Legislation will have to move ahead of the readiness of man to perceive the need. But I believe, if the need is put on the right level, that men are ready for it. What I find missing is the men speaking in democracy's name, who will put it on the right level to people. I think it is always put on the level of personal advantage.

I know perfectly well that Europe today would be a slave continent were it not for America—for her blood and her treasure and her vision. That is a fact. You have done something in history that no other nation has done.

Now it is always put to the American people that it is to your advantage to do it. Well, I don't think so badly of people. What if it were put to the American people that it is to your *disadvantage*—that it means you will have to pull in your belts a bit—but that the whole freedom of humanity depends on America taking this lead? If you have people who put that challenge—and live it—in the White House or Congress, then millions of free men would say: "Yes." But nobody does it. You always think you have to coax a man by appealing to self-interest before he'll do what is right. I don't think so poorly of the common man as that.

Q: Isn't self-interest essential, according to classical economic theory, to make an economic system run?

A: If free men do not learn a new revolutionary concept of unselfishness, they are bound to lose their freedom. And I do not believe it is impossible for free men to be unselfish. Khrushchev said something which in the British press went almost unremarked. In his last big speech in Moscow he made the startling prediction that by the end of this century he believed the Soviets would have a system whereby money was not actually exchanged for goods or services. This seemed so remote from the concept of people in my country that it was not even reported. But I don't take so low a view of human nature as to believe that only selfishness can make it give its best.

The number of people who, in one degree or another, participate in the work of Moral Re-Armament must run into millions. But at the moment there are upwards of three thousand people who do this work full time and give their very best without salary of any kind whatsoever. We share what we have, look after each other's needs, and chip in everything we've got to help each other.

Now I am not so naïve as to think that you will instantly get every big business man or labor leader saying: "I am going to live like that." But if Khrushchev has the vision and the dare to stand before his people and say, "Before the end of this century, we're going to try to create a character in Russia"—that is what it must mean—"whereby we all live in such a way that we don't have to give each other money for what we need," I do not believe it is beyond free men to say: "We'll match that. We will have something far more revolutionary by the end of the century."

Q: If you get the majority of the world trained in Moral Re-Armament, what would happen to the existing economic system in the free world? Would it still be capitalism?

A: Capitalism is fine, but it's no answer to Communism. One is an economic method, the other is an ideology. Communism uses economics, politics, and military might, but I think its basic aim is ideological, to transform the nature of man and society. If you ask me about economic systems, I think the real problem is selfishness. There is enough in the modern world for everybody's need. There is *not* enough for everybody's greed. If people care enough and share enough, everyone will have enough. That has not yet come true in either the Communist or the capitalist world.

Morals and Religion

Q: How are we going to combat the influence of Richard Burton and Elizabeth Taylor? [*Laughter*]

A: I laugh with you, but I don't take it all that amusingly, and I'll tell you why. I have to work in Asia and in Africa. Do you realize that the only America those people in their millions will ever see is what they see on the screen? That, to them, is our world. They'll never come here.

Q: Are we dealing with the real world in talking about morality?

A: I have to deal with the real world all the time. I have to deal with people who very often put on a front of great success, great triumph, while underneath are emptiness and terrible frustration. The world is full of people who do not love their fellow men enough to bring an answer to the sin that binds and blinds them. They tell them, "Don't worry. There's nothing in it," and they send their patients away sick unto death. I'm dealing with a real world because I know that sin can be cured and I want to help my friends, and my enemies if they'll let me, to find a cure for it.

Q: Is Christianity the basis for your ethics?

A: Christ believed in absolute honesty, purity, unselfishness and love. Do the Christians live them? That is the place you have to start if you happen to be a Christian. Otherwise, if you say to a Muslim or a Hindu or Buddhist, "I am a Christian, live like me," they may say, "That is precisely what I'm doing—living like you. I compromise on all my convictions." But if you say to them, "Do you believe in absolute honesty?" they will all say: "Yes." "Then do you live it?" Challenge them to the experimental method. The Almighty will put into their hearts the place where they need to begin. But if you challenge them to that experiment it is as well to have honestly made it first yourself.

Q: What are MRA's relations with the established churches?

A: It challenges them all with their own truth. Moral Re-Armament is something lived. We aim to see that everybody lives it. As a Catholic friend of mine says: "The Church does not need Moral Re-Armament, but Catholics do." That is our attitude to people in the churches. Some of them like it and some of them hate it. We simply take the view that people in the Church should live what they talk about, and we try and hold them to it.

Q: If your message is at heart the basic Christian message, why do any churchmen oppose you?

A: Have you ever tried to tackle a pious, ineffective Christian on the subject of changing and living what he talks about? We have had Christianity preached in Britain for a thousand years, from pulpit after pulpit after pulpit. In terms of the Christian ethic, we have a greater economic advance today than ever before. I thank God for it, and I hope it goes further. But in terms of men's relations with men, communities with communities, older generation with younger generation, we have never been less like the Christian ethic, and we're getting further from it. Something is wrong.

Q: You speak of attacks upon the character of the British people. Is this something new?

A: It is the first time that people have come out openly in the pulpit, in the press, and incidentally on the television, and undermined faith, traditional morality and the standards which we used to accept as normal.

Q: How is the undermining of character being done— specifically?

A: Bishops are standing up in Britain and saying that premarital intercourse is permissible, that God is possibly a myth and it might be a good thing if we didn't mention Him in my country for 25 years. In my boyhood if a bishop had said that, people would have thought he was crazy.

Q: Is this just one bishop, or do you think it is characteristic of the entire religious community?

A: No, it certainly isn't characteristic of the entire religious community, but there is a whole section of the religious leaders of my country who try and keep up with the times by cutting Christ down to human size. In a Christian country that's a very serious thing. I think what sincere Christians and religious people are meant to do is to try and hold the human character up to Christ. If you take Christ as a model for all people, and then make Him conform to human comfort, to human compromise, you attack the character of a nation.

Q: Do you consider Britain a Christian country, and do you consider it important that the world become a Christian world?

A: We're a country that still calls itself Christian, but I think we live far, far from the way a Christian country should live. It should be normal for countries that love freedom to fight to bring Moral Re-Armament to the whole world, because I think freedom can only exist if a certain morality, a certain character exists in people.

Q: Do you think that something like the Profumo scandal could occur in this country, and if it did, would it shake this country as it apparently did Britain?

A: The trouble with America is this: If you love America as she is, which I deeply do, but fight to help her become the country she could be, some people say you are anti-American. Of course I am not such a fool as not to know there are plenty of Profumo scandals behind the curtains in America. You know that as well as I do, and not just in politics. I imagine that if such a thing were discovered in America, there would equally be a fuss. But I'm not at all out to muckrake or point fingers or have a sort of spiritual Gestapo. I'm dead against it. What I want to see is men so love freedom that they will pay the price of extending it in their own country and around the earth.

Q: Do the problems of the world stem from the relationship between man and God or from the broken and destructive relationships between man and man?

A: I think from both. Everybody is guided by something. Some people are guided by money. Some people are guided by power. Some people are guided by what their wives or what their neighbors think. What I want to see is people guided by what you might call the inner voice. There is something everybody has which tells him what's wrong and what's right, and what his relationships should be with his fellow men.

I remember a Liverpool docker who wasn't a Christian. He was a rough old drunk. He began to apply Moral Re-Armament in his home where his family had broken up, and he said a very interesting thing to me. He said: "There are two voices in my heart—a good 'un and a bad 'un. I need to take time each day to throw out the bad 'un and let in the good."

Q: Is the inner voice absolute, or can it be trained or mistrained? What about the Nazi, for example, who obeyed his inner voice and turned in a Jew?

A: The inner voice is very accurate, very down-to-earth and talks your language. It is trained by obedience. But of course you can mistrain it, if you want to. That is why so many church leaders who disbelieve in absolute moral standards, compromise and fail to give the moral direction which is the true job of the Church. They say in effect: "Everybody compromise like us and you'll be more comfortable people to live with."

I don't think that a Nazi who bullied or betrayed a Jew was actually obeying his inner voice. I think he was obeying an ambition to please the boss, and it was the wrong boss. But you don't have to censor the inner voice.

Q: Can you give me a forecast, a prediction? You say we need a massive change of character. Will this happen?

A: I believe it will. We live in an age of the greatest opportunity and greatest danger that ever confronted man. I have faith in the common man in every country. I believe that when he sees that the old, small, deadly hates and fears and greeds that for so long have imprisoned him may actually destroy civilization, he will change. And I believe that change is not only possible, but necessary and even adventurous.

Ideology

Q: You seek to change the individual. If you change the environment, won't individuals change?

A: Mr. Khrushchev said publicly in Moscow, I think in July or August last year, that after years of socialist experiment he has failed to create the new type of man he needs for Communism. I'm passionately keen to change environment, education and institutions, but by themselves they will not change the nature of man.

Q: You speak of Khrushchev attempting to create a new type of man. What does he mean by this new man? Does he mean a man who is just going to be a robot?

A: I think he still hopes new environment will create unselfish men. But from what I hear from inside Russia, he is bitterly up against the fact that his system is not creating them. He says: "We cannot have Stalin. He is debunked. But what can we have?" He has got to have something quickly, or he is going to be pitched out. It is a rough spot to be in.

Have you read *The Emperor of the Blue Ants*? The author is George Paloczi-Horvath and he tells about young Mao Tse-tung in 1917. He writes that Mao was serene, dedicated, a philosopher-athlete. His aim was selfless service of the people. He was completely opposed to any sort of materialism, let alone Marxism. His philosophy was based on absolute moral principles. He yielded these principles because he came to the conviction that power was the one thing that could alter the economic lot of his people.

And then Mao went for power. Stalin was precisely the same. He went for power.

Somehow free men have got to show men like that that it is possible to produce economic and social justice—an economic and social revolution—without force. Otherwise, I think liberty is gone. Or there will be atomic war.

Q: Isn't there a fundamental conflict in the way Khrushchev and you set about creating a new type of man? Your insistence on God, for example?

A: Probably Khrushchev disbelieves in God because he looks at the nations which speak in God's name, and he says: "If there were really a God, they'd be different."

But I don't start on the basis that everybody has to believe in God. I start on the basis that human nature can be changed. I've experienced it. I believe that human nature has got to be changed. That is the root of any permanent world answer. National economies must be changed, that is the fruit of the answer. World history must be changed. Unless we deal with human nature on a colossal scale the world will continue to divide, and possibly destroy itself.

Q: Where do you begin with this great change in human nature?

A: We were talking the other day to some of the most intelligent men in America. One of them said: "Is it intellectual change you are talking about?" And I replied: "Well, if you worship your intellect before God, that's probably where you need to start changing. If you worship dollars or profit or color or class or race or pet hates before you worship God, that's probably where you need to start changing. Everybody knows in his heart where he needs to start. There is no single pattern."

Q: How do you propose creating this new type of man?

A: I'll tell you how you and I can start doing it. Take a piece of paper right now. First, write down four words— "honesty, unselfishness, love, purity." Then put, in very big letters, "ABSOLUTE." Next, if you believe in God, write: "Listen to Him." He'll tell you what to do—how those absolutes apply to you.

If you don't believe in God, be clear how you want everyone around you to live. Be clear in detail. Then start living that way yourself.

Try this experiment. If you try it and it doesn't work, let me know. But if you have honestly tried, you'll be the first person I've met who could say it didn't work.

Finally, be crystal clear what you and I are living for. In the present tumult, where men are technological and industrial giants but moral pigmies, unless we live for the remaking of the world we have an inadequate aim. Because nothing else will save humanity from destruction. It's difficult, but no aim short of that is valid.

Q: How do you reconcile absolute love with your attitude toward the Communists?

A: We need a revolution big enough to include the whole earth, and powerful enough to change the whole earth. When I first began to apply Moral Re-Armament, I told my wife two or three things she didn't know about me. I've always remembered what she said: "Peter, I think I'm meant to love you as you are but to fight to help you become the man you are meant to be."

That is my attitude to Communist and non-Communist alike. I think Communism, which flatly says it cannot triumph until the myth of God is removed from the mind of man, is a narrow idea. I love the Communists enough to try and include them in something far more spacious and far more revolutionary than a narrow class concept.

I am not against Communists. The biggest anti-Communist in history was Hitler. But he only succeeded in spreading Communism over half the earth. I think free men could create a revolution bigger than these class-war men. But do we care enough to do it? We criticize them, but offer no revolutionary alternative. I think that is lack of love.

Q: Why do you refer to only two choices for the world today—Communism or Moral Re-Armament? Why would it not be democracy, for example, opposed to materialism?

A: I think you fail to understand Moral Re-Armament, and, if I may say so, Communism. I single out Communism because it is today, as far as I know, the only idea with a world outlook engaged in a world revolution—apart from Moral Re-Armament.

I respect the sincerity of many Communists and their economic and social achievements. But, by their own admission, they have failed to create a new type of man.

There is a certain level of moral re-armament in everybody in the world—an essence of honesty, purity, unselfishness and love, in leaders and led. Everybody can, if he wants, listen to his conscience, his inner voice, the voice of God. He can become part of a force to turn mankind in the direction God intended men to travel on earth.

DESIGN FOR DEDICATION is set in Linotype Times New Roman, a face designed for the London *Times* in 1931 by a committee of artists and typographers under the supervision of Stanley Morrison. While contemporary in spirit, Times New Roman preserves the elegance and clarity of earlier designs. The dustjacket and display lines are set in Monotype Perpetua, a letter from the hand of Eric Gill, wood engraver and sculptor.

The binding is Joanna Western Blue Untex Gold Stamped

The paper is a 60 lb. special Cream White Scholar Eggshell

The type was set by Service Typographers, Inc., Indianapolis

Printed by Photopress, Inc., Chicago

Typography and design by Robert Borja